Teaching in focus

An ABC of the curriculum

Other titles in this series

Activity methods in the middle years
School-based in-service education

An ABC of the Curriculum

James Eaton

Oliver & Boyd

Oliver & Boyd
Croythorn House
23 Ravelston Terrace
Edinburgh EH4 3TJ

A division of Longman Group Ltd.

ISBN 0 05 002887 1

Set in 10/12pt Photon Times Roman
Printed in Great Britain by The Whitefriars Press Ltd.,
London and Tonbridge

Introduction

This is a sort of Guide Book: it aims to explain in simple words some of the technical and semi-technical terms currently being used in the literature of curriculum development. 'Just what exactly is "Interdisciplinary Enquiry"?' you say, coming across the term, 'If only there were some sort of glossary in which I could look these things up.' Well, here is an attempt to provide one. I have tried to write in easy and readable English, risking the charge of over-simplification if this will enable the reader to find his bearings more easily. To use Bruner's distinction, I have concentrated on economy, perhaps at the expense of power, in an attempt to be clear.

The choice of terms attempts to steer a middle course between the obvious and the obscure. For instance, 'streaming' is too much part of the teacher's stock-in-trade to need explaining, but 'blocked timetable' may not be so familiar. The general area covered is that of Curriculum Design, in particular that of the 'Rational Curriculum Plan', based on the belief that teaching and learning can be improved by the use of a systematic strategy, starting with the formulation of aims and going on from there. Much reference is made to a number of standard authors such as Wheeler, Mager, Bruner, Phenix and Bloom, both to keep the field reasonably compact and also because they are undoubtedly influential writers. Notes on these authors are given in an Appendix.

HOW TO USE THE GUIDE BOOK

Simply look up anything you wish explained. In each entry words in bold type appear as alphabetical items elsewhere in the text, providing a network of cross references. You can thus go through the book in any order you like—it is not designed to be read from A to Z.

List of terms

ACTIVITY CURRICULUM
AFFECTIVE OBJECTIVES
AIMS
ALTERNATIVE SAMPLES
ANALYSIS (Bloom)
APPLICATION (Bloom)
APPROACH RESPONSES
ATTENDING (Bloom)
ATTITUDE(S)
AUTHENTICITY
AUTONOMOUS STUDIES
AUTONOMY
AVOIDANCE RESPONSES

BASIC THEMES
BEHAVIOUR, BEHAVIOURIST
BEHAVIOURAL OBJECTIVES
BLOCKED TIMETABLE
BROAD FIELDS CURRICULUM

CENTRE OF INTEREST
COGNITIVE OBJECTIVES
COMPLEXITY
COMPREHENSION (Bloom)
COMPREHENSIVENESS
COMPULSORY CURRICULUM
CONCEPTS
CONCEPTUAL FRAMEWORKS
CONCRETE OPERATIONAL
   THOUGHT
CONDITIONS OF LEARNING
CONSISTENCY
CONTENT
CONTINUITY
CORE CURRICULUM
CRITERION
CRITICAL PATH
CUMULATIVE SUBJECTS
CURRICULUM
CURRICULUM PROCESS

DIAGNOSTIC EVALUATION
DISCIPLINE(S)
DISCOVERY LEARNING
DOMAIN(S)

ECONOMY
EMPIRICS
ENACTIVE REPRESENTATION
EPISTEMOLOGY
ESTHETICS
EVALUATION (Bloom)
EVALUATION (Curriculum
   Design)
EXPERIENCE

FEEDBACK
FLOW CHART
FOLLOW UP
FORMAL OPERATIONAL
   THOUGHT
FORMATIVE EVALUATION
FORMS OF KNOWLEDGE
FOURFOLD CURRICULUM

GAMING
GOALS
GRAPHICACY

HEURISTIC METHODS
HIDDEN CURRICULUM
HORIZONTAL RELATIONSHIPS

ICONIC REPRESENTATION
IDEOLOGY
INDICATOR(S)
INTEGRATION
INTERACTION
INTERDISCIPLINARY
   ENQUIRY
INTEREST(S)
INTERNALISATION
INTUITIVE APPROACH
INTUITIVE THINKING

KEY CONCEPTS, IDEAS
KNOWLEDGE (Bloom)

LEAD LESSON
LEARNABILITY
LEARNING EXPERIENCE(S)

LOGIC (of a subject)
LOGICAL SEQUENCE

MACRO LEVEL (of
  planning)
MEANINGFUL LEARNING
MICRO LEVEL
MODEL
MOTIVATION

NEEDS
NUMERACY

OBJECTIVES
OBJECTIVE TESTING
OPERATIONAL TERMS
ORACY
ORGANISATION
ORGANISING CENTRES
ORGANISING PRINCIPLE
OVERARCHING AIM

PARADIGM
PARAMETER
PATTERN
PHENOMENOLOGY
POSITIVIST VIEW
POWER
PRINCIPLE LEARNING
PRINCIPLES OF PROCEDURE
PROBLEM CENTRED
  CURRICULUM
PROGRAMMED LEARNING
PSYCHOLOGICAL SEQUENCE
PSYCHOMOTOR OBJECTIVES

RATIONAL CURRICULUM
  PLAN
REALMS OF MEANING
RECALL (Bloom)
RECEIVING (Bloom)
RECEPTION LEARNING
REINFORCEMENT
REITERATION
RELEVANCE

RELIABILITY
REPRESENTATION
REPRESENTATIVE IDEAS
RESOURCES, RESOURCE BASED
  LEARNING
RESPONDING (Bloom)
ROTE LEARNING
ROUTINISATION

SCOPE
SEQUENCE
SIGNIFICANCE
SIMULATION
SOCIOLOGY (of the
  curriculum)
SPIRAL CURRICULUM
STIMULUS
STRUCTURE
SUBJECT-BASED
  CURRICULUM
SUITABILITY
SUMMATIVE EVALUATION
SYLLABUS
SYMBOLIC REPRESENTATION
SYMBOLICS
SYNNOETICS
SYNOPTICS
SYNTHESIS (Bloom)
SYSTEMS ANALYSIS

TAXONOMY
TEAM TEACHING
TECHNOLOGY
THEORY

UTILITY

VALIDITY
VALUE COMPLEX (Bloom)
VALUING (Bloom)
VARIETY
VERIFICATION PROCEDURES
VERTICAL RELATIONSHIPS

ZETETICS

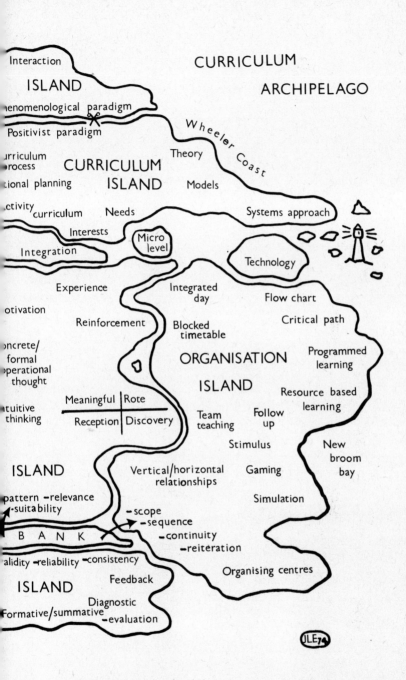

Interaction
ISLAND
Phenomenological paradigm
Positivist paradigm
Curriculum process
rational planning
activity curriculum
Interests
Integration

CURRICULUM
ARCHIPELAGO

Wheeler Coast

Theory
CURRICULUM
ISLAND
Models
Needs
Systems approach

Micro level

Technology

Experience
Integrated day
Flow chart

Motivation
Reinforcement
Blocked timetable
Critical path

concrete/ formal operational thought

ORGANISATION
ISLAND
Programmed learning

intuitive thinking

Meaningful | Rote
Reception | Discovery

Team teaching
Follow up
Resource based learning

ISLAND
Stimulus
New broom bay

pattern –relevance –suitability
Vertical/horizontal relationships
Gaming

–scope
–sequence
–continuity
–reiteration
Simulation

B A N K

validity –reliability –consistency
Organising centres

ISLAND
Feedback

Diagnostic
Formative/summative –evaluation

JLE74

A

Activity curriculum

Some writers distinguish various basic types of curriculum, of which this is one. (See also **core** and **subject curriculum.**) The main sources of its **objectives** are the **motivation** and **interests** of pupils, and its principal feature is its emphasis on active learning, for example through individual and group work, **discovery learning.** The child is regarded as a responsible agent, working at his own pace and following his own bent. Thus a scheme of work for a class pursuing this type of approach might take the form of a **flow chart** developing from a **centre of interest** thus:

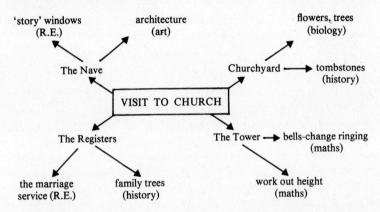

Whether active learning necessarily implies such **organisation** and methods is at least arguable; any real **learning experience,** insofar as it is something the learner *does,* rather than simply *undergoes* is, perhaps, by definition active.

Plowden Report—*Children and their Primary Schools,* ch. 16 (HMSO, London, 1967).

Affective objectives

Bloom's **Taxonomy** divides **objectives** into three areas or **domains,** one of which is the **affective.** The word is derived from psychology, where the term 'affect' is used to refer to emotions, attitudes and feelings, as opposed to cognition, which is to do with thinking and reasoning. This is a useful distinction to make when trying to classify **objectives** according to whether they refer, broadly, to facts or to values. Thus if, say, the aim of a course in Religious Education is that the pupils should develop a sympathetic understanding of Jews, then the **affective objectives** will be those concerned with the aim of developing sympathy.

The second volume of Bloom's **Taxonomy,** edited by Krathwohl, attempts to grade such **affective objectives** from **receiving** or **attending** at the lowest level to characterisation by a **value complex** at the highest, that is from a minimal willingness to learn to a level at which the whole of a person's character is permeated by the system of values aimed at.

This **attitude** scale, though having its uses, is riddled with difficulties. Nevertheless, as a crude scale giving a means of **evaluation** of the degree of commitment shown by pupils towards a given lesson or course, it may have its uses. For instance, a teacher might use it as, say, a five-point scale to record the **interest** shown by pupils: for instance, level 3 (**valuing**) is indicated when a pupil brings to school, say, fossils he collected on holiday.

Aims

Aims, usually linked with **objectives,** are generally taken to be the first step in **curriculum** planning of any kind. We cannot, it is claimed, choose methods, select materials, topics, subject matter, test for success, until our purposes and intentions are settled and stated.

It is useful to make distinction between **aims** and **objectives,** though not all writers do. There are, perhaps, three main ways of going about it. The simplest distinction is one between general and particular. **Aims** are broad statements of intent, such as 'to develop creative thinking'; **objectives** are more specific, such as 'the pupils will be able to distinguish between simile and metaphor'.

A second distinction is that between evaluative and descriptive statements. **Aims** involve making value judgements prescribing or commending something; **objectives** describe what the learner will be able to do when he has successfully completed the learning process. Educational **aims** are connected with values in the field of **knowledge** and understanding; **objectives** are neutral in respect of values.

A third distinction might be put this way: **objectives** are like targets to be shot at, milestones to be passed. An **aim** is more like a signpost or a compass, giving a direction in which to travel, a standard to which to refer. **Aims** thus perhaps cannot be specific, having to do with policy, priorities, strategy, rather than tactics. **Objectives** are not to be derived from them, but only measured against them. This is worth emphasising, as exactness in **aims** is not only unnecessary but also undesirable. They should be used as guidelines, not specifications.

R. S. PETERS, *Authority, Responsibility and Education,* ch. 8, p. 87ff (3rd edition, Allen and Unwin, London, 1973).

Alternative samples

When choosing his teaching topics, constructing his **syllabus,** a teacher may be faced with a very wide range of choice. He cannot cover everything; the explosion of **knowledge** means he must select. The same applies when deciding what should be included in the **curriculum** as a whole. Moreover, with increasing emphasis on raising the level of pupils' thinking, it may be that we have to accept the possibility of reduced 'coverage' in order to allow for this. Thirdly, if **content** is not to be an end in itself but chosen to promote curricular **objectives,** careful selection is important: as well as meeting certain **criteria,** the **content** may have to be pruned, as it were, until there is not too much nor yet too little. Hence the notion of a sample.

For example, to teach pupils to distinguish between religions in respect of their doctrines, ritual, social customs and the like, one teacher might compare Christianity and Judaism, another might choose Islam and Buddhism. If the **aim** of the course is to demonstrate the presence of various dimensions of religious experience, then either sample may serve equally well; the choice may then be made on other grounds, such as the availability of **resources.**

D. K. WHEELER, *Curriculum Process,* p. 200ff (University of London Press, London, 1967).

Analysis

The fourth level of the cognitive **domain** of Bloom's **Taxonomy.** Bloom describes it as 'the breakdown of a communication into its constituent elements or parts such that the relative hierarchy of ideas is made clear and/or the relations between the ideas are made explicit'.

Thus, a pupil who can understand and explain the arguments for and against the building of a new road through an area of natural beauty is probably at this level. A pupil who can identify common elements in the principal Jewish festivals, for example the re-creating of past events in their history, has also progressed to this level. Its distinctive feature, perhaps, is the ability to handle a number of **concepts** or ideas; to keep, as it were, more than one ball in the air at once.

Application
The third level of the cognitive **domain** of Bloom's **Taxonomy.** Bloom describes it as 'the use of abstractions in particular and concrete situations'. Whatever has been understood at level 2 (**comprehension**) is used by the pupil in a new situation. For instance, if he has successfully grasped the idea that metals expand when heated, and then goes on to show in some way that he realises that this must be allowed for in certain types of engineering construction such as bridge building, the pupil is probably learning at this level. He is doing something with the idea—applying it himself, not relying solely on the teacher's initial explanation.

Approach responses
Attitudes themselves, it is widely agreed, cannot be measured. However, if changes in **attitude** are among our **objectives,** how can we tell if we have been successful? Robert Mager suggests that certain features of a person's **attitude** to learning can provide a pretty reliable guide and can, in principle, be measured. Much of what we do can be seen as movement towards, or away from, particular objects, persons or problems, and these movements are a good guide to our **affective** state. A tendency, for instance, to approach members of the opposite sex frequently indicates an **attitude** towards them, and Mager has a disarming and amusing way of pointing this up.

Teachers will recognise the strength of this argument; they know the tell-tale signs of boredom or enthusiasm; but it also has its limitations, **interest** not always being accompanied by overt signs, boredom being often concealed. In any case, this is a very limited **concept** of **attitude**; it is not simply a tendency to court or shun something. *See also* **indicator(s).**

R. F. MAGER, *Developing Attitude toward Learning* (Fearon, Belmont, Calif., 1968).

Attending
The lowest level of the affective **domain** of Bloom's **Taxonomy,** it is also called **receiving.** At this level a pupil's **attitude** towards, say, a history lesson is not, to put it mildly, very developed. He pays attention most of the time, does not spend too much time looking out of the window and is not obviously bored. Hardly an **objective** many teachers will set themselves, except where a class shows a high level of **affective behaviour** in non-approved directions—the pupils have strong **attitudes** all right—unfavourable ones!

Attitude
This word, as used by Robert Mager, means a tendency to **approach** or **avoid** something, a positive or negative **attitude.** For instance 'when we note that a person tends to say "bleaugh!" when faced with an avocado, we might say he doesn't like avocados. When we make such an observation we are making an inference from visible **behaviour** about an internal, invisible condition'.

Here is something which can be clearly specified, which can be measured by the number of **approach responses** and **avoidance responses** the pupil makes. We can devise means of increasing the frequency of the former, decreasing that of the latter, by **reinforcing** or rewarding **approach responses**; by surrounding the subject matter to be learned with pleasant conditions, such as a friendly manner or reasonable expectation of success; or by following it by 'positive consequences' such as approval, helpful comments.

This is an attractive thesis. Mager's racy style is amusing and persuasive. But this **behaviourist** approach should be handled with great care. A fundamental objection to it is that an **attitude** is not simply a tendency to move towards or away from something. An **attitude** is *about* something; it includes a **cognitive** element. **Behaviour** may be very good circumstantial evidence of an **attitude,** but the two are not to be equated. *See* **indicator(s).**

R. F. MAGER, *Developing Attitude toward Learning* (Fearon, Belmont, Calif., 1968).

Authenticity
One of the **criteria** which a given piece of **content** or subject matter should meet if it is to be justifiable. In some authors it is treated as an aspect of **validity,** but it is probably best treated separately. Essentially it asks the question 'is the subject matter in some sense *true*?' In many cases this will mean up to date, not obsolete, so that facts, **concepts** and theories do not have to be unlearned later. In some **disciplines,** however, it may mean true to the **logic** of the subject. A poem 1000 years old may be in some sense **authentic** where one written yesterday is a sham.

Thus, for example, a teacher may have to decide whether to read C. S. Lewis or Enid Blyton to her junior class—or whether one ought to be satisfied with that history book which talks of the Empire on which the sun never sets!

D. K. WHEELER, *Curriculum Process,* p. 219 (University of London Press, London, 1967).

Autonomous studies

One of the elements of the **fourfold curriculum.** In the sense in which it is used by the proponents of that scheme, the phrase refers to subjects which do not 'come through' in **interdisciplinary enquiry.** Mathematics, for instance, is often not easy to teach in an interdisciplinary context and may, therefore, need to be given independent or **autonomous** status in the **curriculum.**

CHARITY JAMES, *Young Lives at Stake,* ch. 6 (Collins, London, 1968).

Autonomy

This has been advanced as a major **aim** of the **curriculum,** and even of education itself. The word implies:

   (a) an ability to see for oneself (auto . . .);
   (b) what the rules are (. . . nomy) of an activity.

The term, in effect, combines the notion of a free, responsible agent—not someone who has been conditioned—with the notion of learning the rules, say, of the **disciplines.** For instance, to learn to understand the rules of mathematics is to learn to think mathematically; to get 'inside' the rules, not simply to follow them blindly. Within these rules, whether of a **discipline** or of a community, there is freedom to act autonomously.

Harris calls autonomy an **overarching aim,** adding that '**autonomy** involves the possession of **knowledge**—without which the **concept** of responsible choice is quite meaningless'.

Open University Course E 283, Unit 8 (Alan Harris).

R. F. DEARDEN, *The Philosophy of Primary Education,* pp. 46–9 (Routledge & Kegan Paul, London, 1968) or in R. S. PETERS (ed.) *Perspectives on Plowden,* ch. 2 (Routledge & Kegan Paul, London, 1969).

Avoidance responses

Like **approach responses,** Robert Mager sees these as evidence of **attitude** to learning, this time negative. People show great ingenuity in finding things to do which put off the moment when they will have to get down to a job they do not much want to do. Thus Mager writes:

'Had you been observing and recording my behaviour when I sat down to complete the third revision of this chapter, your notes might have looked something like this:

   —sat down and turned on electric typewriter
   —turned off electric typewriter
   —went to kitchen for a cup of coffee
   —rearranged papers on desk and sharpened pencils . . . .

It wouldn't really matter what responses you might have seen me make. If the result was to take me further away from the typewriter, you would have been correct to label these avoidance responses.'

R. F. MAGER, *Developing Attitude toward Learning* (Fearon, Belmont, Calif., 1968).

B

Basic themes

When selecting the **content** of a **curriculum** or a course, the subject matter will have to be broken down into larger and smaller units. **Basic themes,** according to Wheeler, come midway between **conceptual frameworks** and **alternative samples.** Examples may make the point: in mathematics—factorising, equations; in chemistry—solubility, acids and bases, oxidation and reduction; in music—rhythm, pitch, harmony; in social studies—man as toolmaker, child rearer, social animal; and so on.

Such themes, or **key concepts, ideas,** are located within the **conceptual frameworks** of the subjects or **disciplines.** The value to the teacher of considering the breakdown of **content** in these terms is that it brings home the need to raise the level of the pupils' thinking above mere **recall** and **rote learning** to the level of understanding such themes, **concepts,** ideas.

D. K. WHEELER, *Curriculum Process*, ch. 8 (University of London Press, London, 1967).

Behaviour, Behaviourist *See* behavioural objectives

Behavioural objectives

Behaviourism is a major branch of the psychology of learning which goes back to the American psychologist J. B. Watson. Perhaps the best-known writer associated with this type of learning theory is B. F. Skinner. According to this school of thought, all learning consists in a relatively permanent change in **behaviour.** This **behaviour** (what the subject does which can be observed in some way—not, be it noted, how he behaves himself!) can be modified and shaped by the teacher or instructor by means of **reinforcement.**

When talking about **objectives,** behaviourist writers insist that they be specified exactly in ways which can be measured—in **behavioural** or **operational** terms. There is much of value in this insistence, if it makes teachers ask themselves what the pupil will be able to do at the end of the week, the term, the course, that he could not at the beginning; but there are many serious objections to this **objectives model** of **curriculum** planning.

For instance, (1) the most important **objectives,** it is said, cannot be specified in this way (for example, appreciation of a poem); again, (2) if **objectives** are set out in this way before we begin to teach, there is little time or room for originality or following up interesting 'red herrings'; (3) it has been argued also that subordinating **content** to this sort of **objective** is in certain cases mistaken; (4) in any case it is impracticable—one would need to list thousands of these **behavioural** changes even in the course of a week's work; (5) perhaps most importantly of all, there are fundamental philosophical difficulties, such as ethical objections to the manipulating of one human being by another. Determinism, responsibility and free will are involved. Skinner, to be fair, is well aware of this last charge, and debates it in his novel, *Walden Two,* which has been described as '1984 through rose-coloured spectacles'.

For objections to behavioural objectives *see Open University Course E 283,* Unit 7, pp. 87–91 (Richard Pring). The novel referred to is B. F. Skinner, *Walden Two* (Macmillan Company, New York, 1969).

Blocked timetable

The traditional secondary school timetable may be a major obstacle to **curriculum** change; **blocking** the **timetable** may be the first stage in breaking up the log jam. A number of teachers, perhaps those in the general area of the Arts, agree to pool their timetable allowance, and ask for, say, one complete afternoon and two double periods per week, during which all the pupils in a year group will be timetabled for this group of subjects. Within this block the teachers concerned may allocate their **resources,** of teachers, rooms, equipment as they think best.

A number of things follow: change to, say, **team teaching** methods is now possible, but it is not obligatory—teaching can go on in the traditional way if desired. There is also a devolution of responsibility;

teachers themselves are involved in timetabling, and can look at various ways in which the time available may be used. Furthermore, the claims of other **curriculum** innovations such as mixed-ability teaching, **integration,** etc. are not ruled out by the timetable.

One limitation of such blocking may be that it makes more difficult links between the areas so delimited; for example, in which block will the R.E. teacher feel most at home, the Arts or the Humanities?

Present opinion and practice seems to be moving towards this basically very simple method of timetabling, and away from the complex programming approach, in which the use of a computer has been seen as the logical conclusion.

JACK WALTON (ed.) *The Secondary School Timetable* (Ward Lock, London, 1972).

Broad fields curriculum
An approach to the **curriculum** through a smaller number of areas than the normal subjects, but not necessarily going as far as, say, **interdisciplinary enquiry.**

C

Centre of interest
Reaction against traditional subject teaching has often led to concentration on the **needs** and **interests** of the pupils. Many teachers, particularly in primary schools, teach by topics rather than subjects. A topic is chosen which children find interesting or which can be developed according to their **interests**; it forms a **centre of interest** from which various interesting investigations may radiate, perhaps leading into areas considerably removed from the original starting point. For some of the arguments for and against this approach *see* **activity curriculum, integration, interests.**

Cognitive objectives

The word 'cognitive' has to do with thinking, knowing (as opposed to feeling and valuing). Thus the cognitive **domain** of Bloom's **Taxonomy** attempts to classify **objectives** of this kind, from the lowest to the highest level, in terms of the **complexity** of the thinking (**organising principle**). The least complex is termed **knowledge** or **recall**; this is thinking without understanding (if that is possible). From here we climb to **comprehension,** the lowest level of understanding; next is **application,** using in a new situation what was grasped at the previous level; **analysis** involves comparing, contrasting, balancing of **concepts,** and similar mental skills; **synthesis** means putting them all together to make one's own picture, as it were; and **evaluation** crowns the pyramid with the ability to make a reasoned judgement on what has gone before.

Whether cognition is so straightforward seems doubtful. Research into this sort of classification in particular subject areas, e.g. history, science, suggests that each **form of knowledge** has its own **logic,** which Bloom's classification may not adequately represent.

Complexity

The **organising principle** of the cognitive **domain** of Bloom's **Taxonomy.**

Comprehension

The second level of the cognitive **domain** in Bloom's **Taxonomy.** It is said to represent the lowest level of understanding. A pupil who can explain a **concept** or idea correctly in his own words is at this level. He does not have to do anything new with it (**application,** level 3) but simply show that he is not merely parrotting or regurgitating the material. For instance, he should be able to explain what he is doing when he squares a number, or puts a metaphor into non-figurative language. It is worth noting that the **concept** itself may be simple or extremely difficult, such as the **concepts** of a rectangle or a rectilinear function. **Comprehension** is not confined to easy **concepts.**

Comprehensiveness

To say that **learning experiences** should meet the **criterion** of **comprehensiveness** is simply to say that there should be enough to meet *all* the **aims** and **objectives** of a course. For example, if one of the **aims** of a course is to develop co-operation, then to have the pupils working as individuals for most of the time is hardly likely to result in the achievement of this particular aim.

Compulsory curriculum

How much of the **curriculum** should be compulsory (if any)? This is a real problem when deciding what should be **core** studies and what optional. At the **macro level** visitors to this country are often astonished that there is no 'official' **curriculum**. In fact only religious instruction is legally compulsory, but there is some force in the argument that at least minimum standards could be demanded by law. Where might such a **core** be found—in the three R's, the four 'aces' (*see* **graphicacy**)? And who would decide anyway?

J. P. WHITE, *Towards a Compulsory Curriculum* (Routledge & Kegan Paul, London, 1973).

Concepts

Much **curriculum** discussion centres round **basic themes, key concepts** and such like. A **concept** or idea may, in effect, be a person's 'mental picture'; for example, my **concept** of an atom is that of a minute billiard ball. But philosophers warn us against such a use of language; to have a **concept** is simply to be able to distinguish one thing from another, say, triangles from other shapes, however one does it.

The point of this talk about **concepts** is once again a reaction against mere regurgitation, **rote learning** without any idea of what one is doing. Moreover, **concepts** in education are not just ideas we pick up as we go along. They are essentially theoretical **concepts,** whether of a **concrete** or **formal operational** kind. To be able to recognise a Gothic arch is to have a **concrete** theoretical **concept; the concept** of a quadratic equation is abstract, or **formal.**

R. F. DEARDEN, *The Philosophy of Primary Education,* ch. 6 (Routledge & Kegan Paul, London, 1968).

Conceptual frameworks

When deciding what the **content** of the **curriculum** should be, at the most general level one is dealing with **forms of knowledge, realms of meaning, disciplines** or some such categories. Within these categories further classification is needed. For instance Literacy may be divided broadly into language studies, literature and communication; Art into creative, performance and appreciative aspects. Mathematics may be thought of in terms of set theory, real and complex number systems, etc.

Within these **conceptual frameworks**—which are by no means clear or agreed—will fit the **key concepts, basic themes.** Such frameworks or conceptual maps are increasingly in evidence in

11

curriculum development, for example the 'Moral Components' of the Farmington Trust; the 'Exploration Man' unit of the Schools Council *Integrated Studies Project*.

D. K. WHEELER, *Curriculum Process,* p. 40 (University of London Press, London, 1967).

Concrete operational thought
The stage of mental development at which, according to Piaget, the child learns to work things out in his head, to 'operate' mentally. He can conserve quantity ('it's the same amount of water, even though it's in a tall jar'); he can reverse a process in his mind. But the **concepts** are still **concrete,** they refer to objects he has experienced through his senses. Thinking at this level is most typical of children in the middle years of schooling.

See, for example, DENNIS CHILD, *Psychology and the Teacher,* ch. 5 (Holt, Rinehart and Winston, New York, 1973).

Conditions of learning
For those who are interested in psychological explanations of how learning takes place, Robert Gagné's book of this name is an important work. He sets out an eight-stage hierarchy of learning processes, from simple conditioning at the lowest level to that of **principles** and problems. For example, Stage 4 is called 'verbal association'; we learn that the French for 'match' is 'allumette' by a verbal linkage, thus: the word 'match' gives us a mental picture of a burning match; this triggers off the associated word 'illuminate', and the syllable 'lum' reminds us of the French word 'allumette'. All this is virtually automatic, in the **behaviourist** tradition; the assumption seems to be that all learning is similar in kind, stimulus being linked to response, but in patterns of ever increasing complexity. The job of the teachers is to facilitate the smooth working of such mechanisms, by careful attention to **motivation, feedback, diagnostic evaluation, structure,** etc.

ROBERT GAGNÉ, *Conditions of Learning* (Holt, Rinehart and Winston, New York, 1965).

Consistency (of Evaluation)
Of the **criteria** which any good test or assessment procedure should meet, this is the one which demands that pupils be tested on what they have actually learned to do; so that, for instance, pupils who have learned to answer short **objective tests** are not assessed on a formal

essay-type examination, in which they have had little instruction or practice.

Content
One of the cardinal points of the **rational curriculum plan.** Sometimes, at the **macro level**, the emphasis seems to be on the overall **structure** of **knowledge**, what should or should not be in the **curriculum**, or how much should be **compulsory**, whether it should be divided into **realms** or **disciplines** or whatever. Sometimes the argument is about the **criteria** which particular items of subject matter should meet to be worth including, or to achieve the **objectives** of a given course (**micro level**).

Continuity
At the stage of the **organisation** of the **content** and **learning experiences** of a course the teacher should bear in mind a number of major factors such as **scope, sequence** and **continuity. Continuity** means that the lessons, topics or **organising centres** should be smoothly linked, so that pupils move easily from one to the next. The teacher whose planning enables him to say 'next week we shall be going on to consider ...' or 'today we are going to develop some variations on ... which we were practising last time' has this **criterion** in mind. Pupils as well as teachers should be able to see the **relevance** and purposefulness of such links.

Core curriculum
This phrase appears to have been little used as such in Britain, but the notion of a 'core' seems to be implicit in a number of curriculum projects. Essentially the idea is that of a central theme or thread which provides the main route, as it were, through the curriculum or part of it. Other topics, areas, subjects can be added, side turnings can be explored, links with other **disciplines** looked for and exploited. Thus, for example, the Schools Council Papers—*Humanities: an approach through Religious Education,* or *History,* or *Classics,* etc., seem to imply the use of such a traditional subject as a 'core' in the humanities area of the curriculum, which can be supplemented by study in associated fields where appropriate.

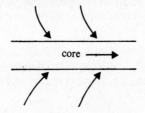

Criterion

Almost too simple a word to include, one might have thought, but perhaps worth having if only to get the spelling right (one **criterion**, many **criteria**). All this word means is a test which something should pass, a standard it should meet. **Criteria** crop up everywhere in **curriculum** development; they set limits of a general kind within which freedom and flexibility is possible and desirable. Thus a proposed set of **learning experiences** should meet such **criteria** as **validity**, **suitability**, etc. No one set is, therefore, the best or correct; the more **criteria** your list satisfies the better. They form a check list; **objectives**, **content, learning experiences** and **evaluation** must all meet the most stringent **criteria** which can be devised. The test of a good course is whether it can withstand this sort of critical appraisal yet remain workable in practice.

Critical path *See* **flow chart**

Cumulative subjects

It is commonly assumed that certain subjects, notably mathematics and languages, are **cumulative**—some would use the word 'linear' or 'sequential' to describe the same notion—that is, the subject matter has to be taken in a relatively fixed **logical sequence**, simple equations before quadratic, indicative before subjunctive, etc. This is sometimes used as an argument against mixed-ability teaching in these subjects. It seems at least worth asking: (i) whether there may not be similar **logical sequences** in all subjects, and (ii) whether the logical conclusion of such an argument is not rather the reverse: where there is such a fixed sequence of **concepts**, pupils will need to work through it at their own individual pace, in which case streaming and setting become a hindrance rather than a help.

Curriculum

Curriculum development of a deliberate kind appears to be a relatively recent phenomenon in Britain; the word **curriculum** itself still rings strange in many ears. Kerr has called it 'all the learning planned and guided by the school', so that it is not only the **content** of courses, the **syllabus**, but also the methods employed, the way the school is organised, the norms and values, the social skills which the school intends its pupils to acquire. (On this basis, be it noted, **hidden curriculum** is a paradox, if not a contradiction in terms.)

Why is this distinction between **curriculum** and **syllabus** considered important? The answer is partly a reaction against regarding subjects as collections of facts, against viewing the **curriculum** as a collection of subjects; and partly it seems designed to force the question of what constitutes an extra-curricular activity, and thus ultimately, perhaps, the crucial question as to which parts of the **curriculum** should be **compulsory**, which parts optional.

J. F. KERR (ed.), *Changing the Curriculum,* esp. ch. 1 (University of London Press, London, 1968).

Curriculum process

D. K. Wheeler's book of this name, perhaps the first comprehensive manual of curriculum design to appear in Britain, outlines a cyclical **model** of **rational curriculum planning**. The distinctive features of this model are:

(a) **Curriculum** planning is a continuous ongoing process.
(b) **Content** is selected *after* **learning experiences** have been planned, and these in turn are chosen to meet specific **objectives**.
(c) **Organisation** is treated as a distinct phase.

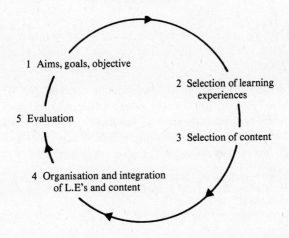

1 Aims, goals, objective

2 Selection of learning experiences

5 Evaluation

3 Selection of content

4 Organisation and integration of L.E's and content

D. K. WHEELER, *Curriculum Process* (University of London Press, London, 1967).

15

D

Diagnostic evaluation

Finding out what a pupil has learned and what he has not, in such a way that difficulties are located, stumbling blocks discovered. When a primary teacher hears a child read, has she a systematic way of recording his errors so as to pinpoint his particular problems? How can a teacher ask questions, set tests which show up which pupils get the correct answers without a clear understanding of what they are doing? To take a simple example:

$$41-$$
$$27$$
$$\overline{}$$

Correct answer 14.

Suppose we ask John to explain exactly how he got this answer, 'Seven from one; can't do it; borrow one' 'Borrow what? Where from? Why?'

This is **diagnostic evaluation**. Many children merely perform a drill mindlessly. How do we find out whether this is so or not?

The more **evaluation** is seen as **feedback** to the pupil and to the teacher, the more likely we are to spot difficulties. **Diagnostic** testing is an aid, not a trap to catch the pupil in failure.

FRED T. WILHELMS, 'Evaluation as Feedback' in Richard Hooper (ed.) *The Curriculum: Context, Design and Development* (Oliver & Boyd, Edinburgh, for the Open University, 1971).

Discipline(s)

In **curriculum** development a **discipline** is a body of **knowledge** with its own rules. Such **disciplines** have come into existence partly because each has its own body of scholars or disciples, partly because they are logically distinguishable from each other. To distinguish between **forms of knowledge, disciplines** and subjects is not easy: mathematics is a **form of knowledge** and a traditional **discipline** in its own right; geography is usually agreed to be a field rather than a **form of knowledge,** but still claims to be regarded not only as a subject but also as a **discipline,** having a respectable academic pedigree, as it were, and its own distinctive **concepts** such as 'zone'. Natural science is usually regarded as a **discipline**, chemistry as a subject. Yet natural science may not be the whole of a **form of knowledge**; psychology is also scientific.

In short, no definitive classification is agreed. Roughly speaking, a **discipline** is something less than a **form of knowledge**, but something more than a subject.

R. C. WHITFIELD (ed.), *Disciplines of the Curriculum* (McGraw Hill, Maidenhead, 1971).
A. R. KING and J. A. BROWNELL, *The Curriculum and the Disciplines of Knowledge* (Rand McNally, Chicago, 1964).

Discovery learning
Discovery learning and discovery-based teaching rest on a belief in the importance of pupils finding out for themselves, not just being told. The teacher provides situations which embody, in implicit or hidden form, **concepts** or **principles** which he needs to acquire. The motto is 'I do and I understand'. Structured apparatus in mathematics and 'Nuffield-type' science experiments use such methods.

Dearden has pointed out some of the limitations of this approach. Theoretical **concepts** are not just lying around waiting to be discovered; the fact that a teacher sees the 'obvious' conclusion is no guarantee that the pupil will do so. Guidance is thus the other side of the coin. Good teaching 'questions, discusses, sets tasks, hints, preserves judicious silences, prompts, provokes, invites contradiction, feigns ignorance, poses problems, demonstrates, pretends perplexity, comments, explains and so on . . . .'

R. F. DEARDEN, *The Philosophy of Primary Education*, ch. 6 (Routledge & Kegan Paul, London, 1968).

Domain(s)
This simply means an area, sector or field. According to Bloom's **Taxonomy**, all **objectives** can be classified into three principal **domains:**

> **cognitive** (thinking, knowing);
> **affective** (feeling, valuing);
> **psychomotor** (physical skills, abilities).

Each of these **domains** is subdivided into a number of levels, according to an **organising principle:**

—in the **cognitive domain,** the **complexity** of the thinking;

17

—in the **affective domain,** the degree of **internalisation** of the **attitude** or value, the extent of the commitment;

—in the **psychomotor domain** no details have been published by Bloom, but Alles suggests **routinisation** as the **organising principle,** the degree to which a given skill becomes a smooth flexible routine.

E

Economy (Bruner) *See* **structure**

Empirics
One of Phenix's **Realms of Meaning.** Clearly this has to do with empirical thinking, thinking based on observable and measurable facts, as typified by the natural sciences. **Knowledge** in this realm comes to us by experience, through the evidence of the senses; the sciences 'provide factual descriptions, generalisations, and theoretical formulations and explanations, which are based upon experimentation in the world of matter, life, mind and society'.

It is not unusual to find people who seem to assume that the 'facts' of the physical world provide us with the only evidence that is strictly dependable, so strong is the grip of the scientific **paradigm.** That this **Realm of meaning** is only one of many seems to come as a surprise to some; facts, it is thought, are facts—all else is opinion. Some fairly modest exploration into **epistemology**—philosophy of knowledge—or even the **sociology** of knowledge is highly desirable for anyone who takes **curriculum** planning seriously.

PHILIP PHENIX, *Realms of Meaning,* Ch. 8–11 (McGraw–Hill, Maidenhead, 1964).

Enactive representation

This phrase of Jerome Bruner describes what happens at that stage of learning which is not yet dependent on mental images—when a child 'learns by the seat of his pants'. There do not seem to be any mental gymnastics taking place, so that this stage is pre-operational, to use Piaget's term. Thus, in the nursery school children's needs may best be met by having plenty of materials to explore, to 'get the feel of': counters of different colours, sizes and shapes, sand, water, etc. Soon this stage will give way to that of **iconic** followed by **symbolic representation**. It has been said that very young children at the first stage know enough of the principle of levers to make a seesaw balance, long before they can 'see', still less explain what they are doing.

JEROME BRUNER, *Toward a Theory of Instruction*, pp. 10–1 (Harvard University Press, Cambridge, Mass., 1966).

Epistemology

The term means philosophy of knowledge, one of the major branches of philosophy having a bearing on **curriculum** planning. The teacher concerned with **curriculum** development is bound sooner or later to have to face, even at a modest level, some basic **epistemological** questions. Two seem particularly important.
1. What is meant by **knowledge**? This is particularly important since **knowledge** is Level 1 of Bloom's **Taxonomy**. To equate it with **recall** seems quite unsatisfactory; something like this seems required:
   'I know something' means:

   (a) I believe it; I understand what I am saying;
   (b) It is in fact true; I cannot *know* that the earth is flat;
   (c) I have some sort of acceptable evidence for it, my own experience or a recognised authority.

   The word 'know' is, therefore, correctly used only if all these apply—otherwise it may be a case of, for example, true belief (a) + (b). In the Bloom sense neither (a) nor (c) is required.

   The moral? We must teach for understanding by the use of evidence if **knowledge** is our aim. (This is perhaps why religious education is such a thorny subject—what counts as evidence for religious claims?)
2. Are there, as Hirst claims, different **forms of knowledge** and understanding? This will depend on how we test for truth in, say, art or mathematics. It is arguable that the philosophy of his subject

19

must be part of a teacher's education. For example, it can make a lot of difference to one's teaching whether one regards history as one of the social sciences or not; some grasp of the philosophy of science is essential if we are to educate pupils into scientific thinking.

For a brief discussion of both questions *see* J. GRIBBLE, *Introduction to Philosophy of Education,* ch. 3 (Allyn and Bacon, Boston, 1969).

Esthetics

Spelled in this way the word refers to one of Phenix's **Realms of Meaning**. (Aesthetics usually means philosophy of art.) Included in this realm are music, the visual arts, the arts of movement, and aspects of literature. 'Meanings in this realm' says Phenix, 'are concerned with the contemplative perception of particular significant things as unique objectifications of ideated subjectivities'! This rather awesome sentence suggests a number of ways in which the arts differ from other disciplines:

(a) the uniqueness of the work of art; the artist does not seek to generalise as, say, a scientist does;
(b) the artist is concerned with the formal properties of his work, its shape, pattern, texture, composition, etc.;
(c) the artist attempts to make objective (outside himself, public) something of his own subjective views and/or feelings.

An interesting point is whether the aim of art in the **curriculum** is to enable pupils to create works of art or merely to understand them—is the latter possible without the former, anyway? Do you have to create to be artistic?

PHILIP PHENIX, *Realms of Meaning,* ch. 12–15 (McGraw-Hill, Maidenhead, 1964).

Evaluation (Bloom)

This is the highest level of the cognitive **domain** of Bloom's **Taxonomy** involving, for instance, 'judgements about the value of material and methods for given purposes'. To give a simple example: a pupil has shown that he can compare and contrast the argument for and against abortion, or the siting of a factory, or even putting up the rates (**analysis**). Furthermore, he can produce an argument for and against similar problems (**synthesis**). To show evidence of understanding at the level of **evaluation** he must be able to assess the weight of these relative cases, detect weaknesses in the reasoning where they exist, and show where the balance of the evidence points.

Traditional essay questions often aim at this sort of product, though they rarely evoke it.

Evaluation (Curriculum Design)

One of the four cardinal points of **rational curriculum planning** in its orthodox form: **objectives; content; learning experiences; evaluation.** A number of points may be very briefly made.

1. **Evaluation** includes measuring and assessing, but also involves an element of judgement of value over and above the facts established.
2. **Evaluation** may be of pupils and their work, the extent to which objectives were realised by the pupils; or it may be course evaluation, a review of the **curriculum** design itself—how good were the **learning experiences**, the **content**, the **objectives**, the **evaluation** procedures themselves?
3. Pupil **evaluation** may rank pupils in order along some scale; or it may test their achievement against some fixed standard; or it may be designed to be **diagnostic**. (Which of these does/did the Eleven Plus do?)
4. **Evaluation** may be **summative** (at the end of a course) or **formative** (continuous, ongoing).
5. **Evaluation**, like other aspects of **curriculum** planning, should meet various **criteria**, such as **validity, consistency, reliability, objectivity**.
6. **Evaluation** is best seen as **feedback**, both to the teacher as a guide to his teaching and planning, and to pupils as an aid to enable them to succeed, not to point out and emphasise failure.
7. Not all **aims** and **objectives** are easy to evaluate, **affective objectives** in particular. There is a temptation to place most of the emphasis on what can be easily measured, the cognitive **domain**, particularly its lower levels.

The crucial problem in pupil **evaluation** seems to be that of meeting as many as possible of the **criteria** referred to or implied above, while at the same time devising a system that is workable, simple to operate, and not unduly time-consuming. Teaching must also determine what is to be tested, not vice-versa. **Evaluation**, in a word, is a good servant but a bad master.

S. WISEMAN & D. PIDGEON, *Curriculum Evaluation* (N.F.E.R., Windsor, 1972).
Evaluation in Curriculum Development: Twelve Case Studies—Schools Council Research Studies (Macmillan, London, 1973).

Experience *See* **learning experience**

F

Feedback

A term derived from cybernetics, the science of controlling processes. The principle is one whereby some of the energy used in a process is diverted to control it in some way. This can be negative **feedback**, which reverses the process as in, say, a cistern which empties itself automatically when full and then begins to fill up again; or it can be positive as in, say, a machine gun, where some of the explosive force is directed to reload and refire, to continue the process.

Testing and **evaluation** are coming more and more to be thought of as **feedback**; a test can be a teaching method, as knowledge of results is known to be a strong **motivator**, especially when it is immediate. If such tests are **diagnostic**, so much the better.

F. T. WILHELMS, 'Evaluation as Feedback', in Hooper (ed.), *The Curriculum: Context, Design and Development* (Oliver & Boyd, Edinburgh, for the Open University, 1971).

Flow chart

A particular type of **model** for planning; a way of setting out in diagram form the sequence to be followed when a number of decisions have to be taken, and one decision depends on another. Thus, for example, a Headmaster contemplating going over to a **blocked timetable** might plan as in Flow Chart (a).

This is obviously a fairly simple example which could be done in one's head, but a more complex sequence might need setting out in order to avoid muddle. This is part of that approach to **curriculum** planning known as **systems analysis**, which also includes, for instance, the notion of **critical paths**. For example, when planning a topic in a fifth form social studies course, the procedure could be set out as in Flow Chart (b).

The **critical path** is the longest time needed for planning, in this case C–F–G. The planning must start at least six months beforehand if the unit depends on a film which has to be booked that far ahead.

For examples of and discussion of the **systems analysis** approach *see Open University Course E 283*, Unit 9 (which is hard going), or R. G. CAVE, *An Introduction to Curriculum Development*, ch. 5 (Ward Lock, London, 1971); also J. E. MERRITT, *What shall we teach?* (Ward Lock, London, 1974).

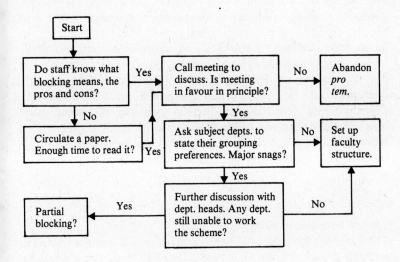

Flow Chart (a)

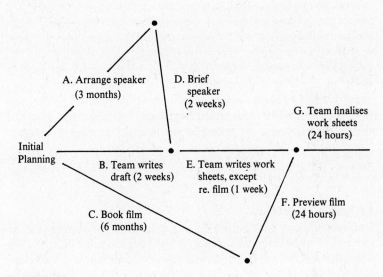

Flow Chart (b)

Follow up
Presumably derived from games—a kick ahead gains no ground unless followed up—this term is commonly found when courses being planned depend on some sort of initial starter, **stimulus** or **lead lesson**, as in **team teaching**. Some **learning experiences** such as films, television programmes, visiting speakers, may be of limited value if not followed up. If learning consists largely of developing new **concepts**, these are only firmly grasped if the learner can do something with them, 'translate' them in some way. (See **comprehension**.) He needs practice to do this, so that he learns actively. Thus **follow up** is not just desirable but essential; otherwise there is no way of evaluating whether any learning has taken place at all.

DAVID WARWICK, *Team Teaching,* ch. 5 (University of London Press, London, 1971).

Formal operational thought
The Swiss psychologist Jean Piaget talks of **formal thought** following **concrete thought** usually some time in the early 'teens, the age varying from child to child and subject to subject. A 'mental operation' is a process in which one works something out in one's mind, a sort of mental manipulation. If that something can be experienced by the senses (e.g. a train, a telephone), we have a **concrete operation**; if what we are thinking of cannot be experienced by the senses (e.g. a cosine, a civil right, the idea of counterpoint), we are abstracting and the operations are **formal**. A pupil at the age of eleven, for instance, is likely to say that a chemical reaction is 'something that happens pretty quick'; he has a **concrete** idea in mind. At fourteen he may say it is 'an expected or unexpected happening between more than one thing'. He has begun to generalise, to abstract, to think formally.

For a brief account of Piaget's theory of Concept Formation *see,* for example, DENNIS CHILD, *Psychology and the Teacher,* ch. 5 (Holt, Rinehart and Winston, New York, 1973).

Formative evaluation
Evaluation which goes on during a course or project, rather than at the end of it. Military intelligence, it has been said, is not much use when the war is over. In pupil **evaluation** the watchword is **feedback**; in course **evaluation** 'the greatest service **evaluation** can perform is to identify aspects of the course where revision is desirable' (Scriven in *Curriculum Evaluation,* AERA *Monograph Series on Curriculum Evaluation* No. 1, Rand McNally, Chicago, 1967). One problem is, perhaps, for teachers to persuade themselves that criticism is not to be

taken personally but is a vital part of the planning process. Whether in a prestigious Schools Council project or a school-based course, it is hard to admit failure.

S. WISEMAN & D. PIDGEON, *Curriculum Evaluation* (N.F.E.R., Windsor, 1972).

Forms of knowledge, understanding

This term is closely associated with Professor Paul Hirst of Cambridge. The **curriculum** is overcrowded, many subjects competing for inclusion. Should someone decide on those subjects or **disciplines** which are of central importance, perhaps even making them a **compulsory core**? Alternatively, might one try to pick out a number of 'ways of looking at the world'? To think mathematically is not the same as to think scientifically; to understand the world as an artist is different again. Hirst claims that there are about half a dozen such **forms**, each with:

(a) its own network of **concepts**—mathematicians don't talk about sin nor artists about variables;
(b) its own way of establishing truth: mathematicians demonstrate proofs, scientists experiment, hypothesise, etc. (**verification procedures**).

Such **forms** include, according to Hirst: (i) formal logic and mathematics; (ii) the physical sciences; (iii) understanding of our own and others' minds; (iv) moral judgements; (v) aesthetic experience; (vi) religious belief; (vii) philosophical understanding.

P. H. HIRST & R. S. PETERS, *The Logic of Education,* ch. 4 (Routledge & Kegan Paul, London, 1970).

Fourfold curriculum

The Curriculum Laboratory of Goldsmiths College, London University has, led by Charity James, pioneered the notion of a revolutionary secondary **curriculum** with four main areas: **interdisciplinary enquiry; autonomous studies**; remedial education; special interest studies. Of these, **interdisciplinary enquiry** has taken root in some form in quite a number of schools. An account of how one school rethought its entire **curriculum** along these lines can be found in chapter 6 by W. F. Clarke (Head of St Helier Boys' School, Jersey) of David Warwick (ed.), *Integrated Studies in the Secondary School* (University of London Press, London, 1973).

CHARITY JAMES, *Young Lives at Stake* (Collins, London, 1968).

G

Gaming

A game has been defined as any contest played according to rules and decided by skill, strength or apparent luck. Apart from the point about rules, perhaps the most important feature of a game is that it is not the real thing; it is non-serious in the sense that it is apart from the actual business of living. But it may prepare us for real life situations without the risks which may accompany mistakes in real life. You can go bankrupt in *Monopoly* without it really hurting. Thus children may discover by means of a geographical game, for instance, why an oil terminal is to be sited at a particular place.

The difference between **gaming** and **simulation** is perhaps one of emphasis. In **gaming** one is learning to handle rules and procedures; in **simulations** we are setting up a simplified 'let's pretend' situation— the participant experiences what it is like to be in a certain situation.

P. J. Tansey & Derick Unwin, *Simulation and Gaming in Education* (Methuen, London, 1969).

Goals

A **goal** in **curriculum** development is to be found somewhere between an **aim** and an **objective**. Wheeler makes a lot of use of the term in **Curriculum Process**, further subdividing **goals** into ultimate (long term), mediate, and proximate (short term) **goals**. The point at which an **objective** becomes a **goal**, a **goal** an **aim**, is nowhere laid down and

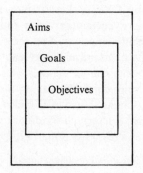

probably does not matter much. One might speak of the **objectives** of a lesson, the **goals** of a course and the underlying **aims**, which (*see* **aims**) are rather more like general statements of intention or direction.

D. K. WHEELER, *Curriculum Process*, ch. 5 (University of London Press, London, 1967).

Graphicacy

This concept is an interesting addition to the ideas of literacy, **numeracy** and **oracy** (or articulacy) which appear to have entered the educational vocabulary in the 1960's; it has been claimed that it should be the 'fourth ace in the pack' (of educational **aims**?).

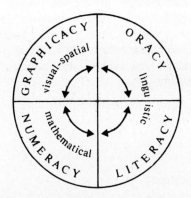

KEITH WHEELER, 'Geography' in Richard Whitfield (ed.), *The Disciplines of the Curriculum*, ch. 6 (McGraw-Hill, Maidenhead, 1971).

H

Heuristic methods

This means much the same as **discovery** methods, and is derived from the same Greek root as Archimedes' 'Eureka'.

Hidden curriculum

The term seems originally to have been coined by the American writer P. W. Jackson. What children learn in school is often very different from what it is intended they learn. They learn to cope; how to create a good impression; how and when to cheat (what is working together in Mr X's class is cheating in Mr Y's); they learn to accept the authority of people other than parents; they learn to be failures if they do not make the grammar school or the top sets; they learn that Vb2 is 'really' Vd.

Is such a **curriculum** 'planned and guided by the school'? **Sociology** has worked hard at this thesis: what happens in classrooms has become the **phenomenology** of the **curriculum**; the implication sometimes seems to be that deliberate **curriculum** planning is a cover-up, if not a complete waste of time. This may breed cynicism about the possibility of **curriculum** reform, but it may also open our eyes to the constraints under which teachers work; education, like politics, is the art of the possible.

P. W. JACKSON, *Life in Classrooms* (Holt, Rinehart & Winston, New York, 1969).
Open University Course E 283, Unit 5, 'The Curriculum, the Teacher and the Child' (John Raynor).

Horizontal relationships

Diagrams of schemes of work or courses are often set out so that they read up the page, thus, say:

	History	Geography
Year 3	Normans	Africa
Year 2	Vikings	Europe
Year 1	Romans	Britain

Horizontal relationships are those across the page, i.e. in this case between history and geography. Year 1 history could well be linked with geography at certain points, say with reference to communications. Such links may be fairly loose, or the two subjects may be **integrated**. The link may be one of agreed common **objectives** or **learning experiences** such as project-based work, and so not necessarily obvious from the course **content**. Wheeler refers to this as the **scope** of the **curriculum**, and it is an important aspect of the **organisation** stage of **curriculum process**.

AUDREY & HOWARD NICHOLLS, *Developing a Curriculum,* p. 65 (Allen & Unwin, London, 1972).

I

Iconic representation
According to Jerome Bruner this mode of **representation**, this way in which we form **concepts**, follows the **enactive** stage and is succeeded by the **symbolic** mode. At the **iconic** stage children 'come to recognise a visualisable path or pattern'. This has not yet been put into words or symbols, but there is a mental picture ('ikon' means likeness); the 'penny drops'. According to Bruner we learn a lot this way, without language or reasoning being involved.

Although words are central to teaching and learning, we should make good use of the power of mental images. A Venn diagram (*see* **interests** for a simple example) is easier to grasp than the same idea in words. Children who have difficulty in distinguishing *b* from *d* can sometimes be helped by a picture of a bed ('see the bedposts?'). It is not coincidence that when we understand something really well we say 'ah, I see!'

JEROME BRUNER, *Toward a Theory of Instruction,* p. 10 (Harvard University Press, Cambridge, Mass., 1966).

Ideology
A socially founded thought-system, such as elitism or egalitarianism. **Ideologies** have a powerful influence on our view of the **curriculum**. *See* **sociology of the curriculum**.

Open University Course E 282, Unit 14, 'Ideologies and Education' (Cosin).

Indicators

It is fairly clear that **attitudes** themselves cannot be measured. Yet an **attitude**, like an intention, is closely tied up with what one does, and what one does is observable. Thus frequent use of the library is probably a good indicator of an **interest** in, an **attitude** towards, books; it could also, of course, indicate **interest** in the librarian, but we could check this by other **indicators**. The point of putting in this item is to suggest that such **indicators** may help teachers to assess **affective objectives**: which voluntary clubs does she belong to? How much time does he spend checking work before handing it in? A simple pupil profile under such headings as co-operativeness, care, commitment can, if based on a systematic attempt to make use of such **indicators**, form the basis of a quite sophisticated **evaluation** of **attitudes**.

ROBERT MAGER, *Developing Attitude toward Learning, passim* (Fearon, Belmont, Calif., 1968).

Integration

Potentially a confused and confusing area—let us attempt some simplification. **Integration** means the breaking down of barriers; a given person's definition may depend on which barrier he wants removed. We may set the field out thus:

Barrier to be broken down between	Possible results
A. Subject matter/**disciplines**. All knowledge is one	**Integration** of **content**
B. Lesson divisions. Away with bells!	Integrated day
C. Children. No such thing as sheep and goats	Non-streaming; mixed ability teaching
D. Teachers. End teacher isolation	**Team teaching;** planning
E. Teachers and pupils. All are learners. Down with authoritarianism!	Loose authority structure; democracy; christian names all round
F. Classrooms. Away with artificial partitions	Open plan buildings
G. Teaching groups. The notion of a school class is outdated	Flexible grouping; individual timetabling

One could add others. The point is that it is not necessary to buy the whole package. For example, although many of those who talk of **integration** refer to subject matter (A), first-school teachers tend to associate the word with (B), and do not necessarily include (A)—they have a number corner, science project, etc. They may, in fact, be quite conservative in their views of the **content** of the **curriculum**.

Where **integration** does refer to the subject matter, problems of **epistemology** arise, questions concerning the desirability of a **subject-based curriculum**. Proponents of **integration** have sometimes been anti-intellectual, against the aridity of the traditional **curriculum** of, say, the Grammar school as they see it, yet they have wished to replace it with something of a mish-mash, where **knowledge** is undifferentiated. This argument has now been pretty effectively demolished so that, for instance, the Schools Council Integrated Studies Project states quite clearly that it advocates what has come to be known as **interdisciplinary enquiry**, which implies that there are many different ways of looking at a common theme or topic.

CHARITY JAMES, *Young Lives at Stake,* ch. 6 (Collins, London, 1968).
RICHARD PRING, 'Curriculum Integration' in Richard Hooper (ed.) *The Curriculum: Context, Design and Development* (Oliver & Boyd, Edinburgh, for the Open University, 1971).

Interaction

Used loosely, this term is coming to replace what used to be called class management. In fact, however, a good deal of research has been carried out recently on the way teachers and pupils act and react to each other, and between themselves in classrooms. Researchers have recorded the amount and type of teacher talk; teacher's questions, for instance, have been classified as 'open' or 'closed' (does the teacher want a specific answer or not?); traditional classrooms need different teaching styles from open plan areas; non-verbal communication has a powerful influence on learning, etc.

D. BARNES, *Language, the Learner and the School* (Penguin, Harmondsworth, 1969).
D. H. HARGREAVES, *Interpersonal Relations and Education* (Routledge & Kegan Paul, London, 1972).

Interdisciplinary enquiry

This term, associated with Charity James, of the Goldsmiths College Curriculum Laboratory, London University, has come to be known as I.D.E., and is one of the four elements of a proposed reconstruction of the secondary **curriculum**, the others being **autonomous studies,** remedial education and special interest studies, the whole comprising the **fourfold curriculum**.

I.D.E. is teaching focused on themes or problems, which need to be looked at from the point of view of more than one **discipline**, in an enquiry-based approach. Though few schools have taken to it wholesale (its proponents would claim up to 50% of the timetable), the rationale has been influential.

I.D.E. is not to be confused with **integration** of subject matter. Various **disciplines**, each with its own tools of enquiry, work together on a common theme or problem. Teachers can remain scholars in specialist **disciplines**. One will say 'as a biologist I see it this way'; another can add 'don't forget the moral (or aesthetic) factors involved'. In I.D.E., it is claimed, the pupil can acquire 'an armoury of possible symbolic systems'.

CHARITY JAMES, *Young Lives at Stake,* ch. 6, esp. pp. 141ff. (Collins, London, 1968).

Interests

The phrase '**needs** and **interests**' (teaching to be based on, etc.) has become something of a cliché. What does it mean? It may help to make a few simple distinctions.

1. Some things are in children's **interests** to learn (A). Children are interested in some things (B). We should teach as much as possible from the overlapped area (A + B).

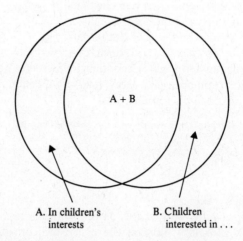

A + B

A. In children's interests   B. Children interested in . . .

2. What children are interested in is not fixed; good teaching can and should create **interest**.

3. If children are not interested they will not learn as effectively as if they are.
4. An **interest** is not just a feeling of enthusiasm. Initial **stimulus** does not create **interest**, it only opens the gates; you become interested as you 'get the hang of it'.

For fuller treatment *see* P. S. WILSON, *Interest and Discipline in Education*, ch. 2 (Routledge & Kegan Paul, London, 1971).

Internalisation
The **organising principle** of the **affective domain** of Bloom's **Taxonomy**.

Intuitive approach
A possible alternative to the **rational curriculum plan**. Imagine a teacher whose **aims** are clear, and who may have in mind certain **principles of procedure, criteria**, standards, but who rejects the notion that **content** and **learning experiences** need to be planned in advance. Such a teacher capitalises on what turns up, a topic in the news, something a pupil brings to school. **Structures** are then 'emergent, the consequence of **interaction** between pupils, teachers and others'.

MALCOLM SKILBECK, 'Openness and Structure in the Curriculum', in P. H. TAYLOR & JACK WALTON, *The Curriculum: Research, Innovation and Change* (Ward Lock, London, 1973).

Intuitive thinking (Piaget)
The stage which precedes **concrete operational** thinking in Piaget's developmental account of children's thought. It is said to cover the years four to seven. Children's conceptual thinking is rudimentary; for instance, they lack conservation, and assess quantities on their most obvious appearances. Boy B in the picture is taller than boy A; there are more balls in line A than in line B.

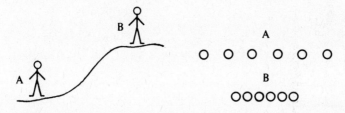

DENNIS CHILD, *Psychology and the Teacher*, ch. 5 (Holt, Rinehart & Winston, New York, 1973).

K

Key concepts, ideas *See* **basic themes**

Knowledge (Bloom)
In Bloom's **Taxonomy** this is the lowest level in the **cognitive domain**, that is the area of thinking and understanding. It is also referred to as **recall,** a less misleading title (*see* **epistemology**) as there is considerable doubt about the claim of this sort of **behaviour** to be called **knowledge**. 'If one thinks of the mind as a file', says Bloom, 'the problem in a **knowledge** test situation is that of finding in the problem or task the appropriate signals, cues and clues which will most effectively bring out whatever **knowledge** is filed or stored'.

No understanding is required, it is implied. Philosophers will have none of this; if a child knows, say, what the capital of France is, he must logically understand something of what 'capital' means. Nevertheless, it seems undeniable that many children do **recall** facts at this level, and that it may not be a completely valueless exercise. But to call it **knowledge** is rather unfortunate.

For a not too difficult analysis of the problem referred to *see* JAMES GRIBBLE, *Introduction to Philosphy of Education,* p. 56ff (Allyn and Bacon, Boston, 1969).

L

Lead lesson
A term much used in **team teaching**. A large number of pupils, perhaps a year group, is given a specially prepared lesson, normally by one of

the teaching team, chosen because he is a specialist on that particular topic or a good performer with a large audience. These lessons must not be too long, they should be varied in format, and they must be good, making use of whatever **resources** are available—films, overhead projector transparencies, tape recordings, etc. These **lead lessons** need **follow up** in smaller groups so that the learning can be an active process.

DAVID WARWICK, *Team Teaching,* ch. 5 (University of London Press, London, 1971).

Learnability (*See* **logical** and **psychological sequence**)

On the face of it this term hardly needs explaining. It is one of the **criteria** to be applied to the proposed **content** of a course. Is the subject matter pitched at a level at which the pupils can understand it?

Yet much of what we teach is not within the pupils' grasp; it may depend on **concepts** requiring **formal operational thinking**, which pupils at the **concrete operational** stage cannot handle. Even simple words like 'tend' (as in 'this tends to happen') can be a stumbling block. Or the level of explanation may be right, but the **concept** may not link with what the pupil already knows. You cannot teach the school team to play the offside trap if some of them do not properly understand 'offside'. Can you learn the concept of a 're-entrant' if you do not understand 'contour'?

Learning experience(s)

A cardinal point of the orthodox form of the **rational curriculum plan: objectives; content; learning experiences; evaluation.** Some brief points:

(a) the phrase is preferable to 'methods' in that it concentrates attention on what the pupil does;

(b) **learning experiences** should meet a number of **criteria**, such as: **validity, comprehensiveness, variety, pattern, relevance to life**;

(c) the literature on the teaching-learning process is enormous; the reader is referred to: **conditions of learning, discovery learning, enactive, iconic** and **symbolic representation, gaming, interaction, interest(s), intuitive, concrete** and **formal operational thinking, meaningful learning, motivation, needs, logical** and **psychological sequence, reinforcement, structure**;

(d) 'experience' implies activity of some kind—it is not simply something that happens. *Verb. sap.*

D. K. WHEELER, *Curriculum Process,* ch. 6–7 (University of London Press, London, 1967).

Logic (of a subject)

To most people the idea of **logic** suggests, if not Mr Spock of Star Trek, the sort of exercise in which all men are mortal; I am a man, therefore I must be mortal. This is part of formal **logic** and goes back

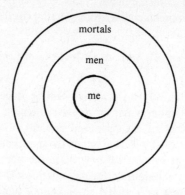

to Aristotle. The **logic of a subject**, or a **form of knowledge**, however, 'refers to the principles which decide whether or not particular intelligible claims to know something are true or false' (Gribble, p. 51). In this sense mathematics is logically distinct from science, though scientists *use* mathematics. Morality has a different **logic** from that of religious belief. Perhaps education does not flower until the pupil begins to see something of these **logical** differences; to realise, for example, that the existence of God is not to be scientifically proved or disproved, or that in environmental studies science, morality and art pose different sorts of questions.

JAMES GRIBBLE, *Introduction to Philosophy of Education,* ch. 3 (Allyn and Bacon, Boston, 1969).

P. H. HIRST & R. S. PETERS, *The Logic of Education,* ch. 4 (Routledge & Kegan Paul, London, 1970).

Logical sequence

Which is preferable, to say 'the Capital city of a country is where the Government or Parliament meets. Let us look at some examples: London, Washington, Canberra...' or 'London is the capital of Britain, Washington of the U.S.A., Canberra of Australia. Now what have they in common?'

It has been suggested that the former is the **logical**, the latter the **psychological sequence**—the order of discovery—rules being derived from instances, not vice versa. The second way, moreover, is better in that it enables pupils to abstract from concrete facts, to generalise.

And it is true that we do learn, in the main, from our experience. Yet 'because of historical facts, exposition and the deductive mode of thought have had the greatest authority in schools' (Wheeler).

But both deductive (examples from rules) and inductive thinking (rules from instances) are equally **logical**; the **logical-psychological** controversy is misconceived; it depends on how we wish pupils to learn in a given situation.

D. K. WHEELER, *Curriculum Process*, pp. 242–3 (University of London Press, London, 1967).

M

Macro level (of planning)
The derivation of this current jargon phrase is unclear; it seems simply to refer to large scale, 'macroscopic', planning as, for instance, in the work of the Schools Council or at Government or Local Authority level; it could also refer to study of the **curriculum** which includes consideration of major social factors such as pressure groups, political **ideologies**, etc.

See, for example, *Open University Course E 283*, Unit 5 'The Curriculum, the Teacher and the Child' (John Raynor).

Meaningful learning
An interesting account of different modes of learning is given by David Ausubel, something as follows:

	Reception	Discovery
Rote	C	D
Meaningful	A	B

Meaningful learning is what it says—learning with understanding. It can be (A) **reception learning**, where the entire content of what is to be learned is presented to the learner in its final form, or (B) **discovery learning**, where the learner unravels the **structure** for himself. Its opposite is **rote learning**, which is little more than conditioning, but which can also occur as (C) **reception** or (D) **discovery learning**—as when one discovers the right answer in mathematics by a happy accident; the learner realises what he has learned, yet has little if any idea of how he got there.

D. P. AUSUBEL, *Educational Psychology* (Holt, Rinehart & Winston, New York, 1968), also in E. STONES (ed.), *Readings in Educational Psychology,* p. 193ff (Methuen, London, 1970).

Micro level (of planning)
Planning, or study of the **curriculum** on a small, 'microscopic', scale as, for instance, in the classroom, in the school. This is the level with which most readers of this book are likely to be concerned.

Model
In **curriculum** development a **model** is usually a simplified diagrammatic layout of some explanation or **theory** concerning a situation or problem which is considerably more complicated. The **theory** is reduced, as it were, to its bare bones, and the skeleton laid out for anatomical inspection. Tyler's simple **model** (R. W. Tyler: *Basic Principles of Curriculum and Design,* University of Chicago Press, 1949), for instance, poses with great **economy** the questions which together need forty words to say in prose:

Aims and Objectives
↓
Content
↓
Organisation
↓
Evaluation

1. What educational purposes should the school seek to attain?
2. What educational experiences can be provided that are likely to attain these purposes?
3. How can these educational experiences be effectively organised?
4. How can we determine whether these purposes are being attained?

Wheeler's 'wheel' **model** in **Curriculum Process** (University of London Press, 1967) is another well known example, as is Kerr's in *Changing the Curriculum* (University of London Press, 1968).

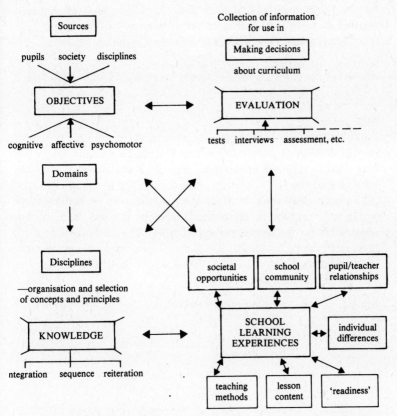

* Reproduced from *Changing the Curriculum* by John F. Kerr with the permission of the University of London Press.

Two further points should be considered.

1. Some models explain what happens; they are descriptive, **models** *of* something. Other **models** are prescriptive, setting out strategies or procedures; **flow charts** are like this; Kerr's **model** *for* Curriculum Theory seems to imply such an approach.

2. A **model** only gives the outline to be filled in; the bones need covering in flesh. Details will vary according to the particular situation. Everyone has a skull, but my face is rather less attractive than the Mona Lisa's.

One other thought worth the quotation: '**Models** are undeniably beautiful and a man may be justly proud to be seen in their company. But they may have hidden vices. The question is, after all, not only whether they are good to look at but whether we can live happily with them' (A. Kaplan, *The Conduct of Enquiry,* Chandler, 1964).

For a clear account of some current models *see* DENIS LAWTON, *Social Change, Educational Theory and Curriculum Planning* (University of London Press, London, 1973).

Motivation

Pupils will not learn well unless they are motivated, unless they want to. The subject is complex, but one can make a broad distinction between (a) extrinsic **motivation**, that of **reinforcement**—what has been termed the K.I.T.A. theory, the kick in the arse approach, and (b) intrinsic **motivation**, in which success is its own reward, the pupil works well because he understands what he is doing, and is made responsible for his own standards of work. This is most likely if the tasks set involve 'cognitive dissonance'—just hard enough to make the pupil think 'I know I can do this if I stick at it'. Too easy and he gets bored; too hard and he gives up.

RONALD MORRIS, *The Quality of Learning* (Methuen, London, 1951)—dated (?) but good reading.

Needs

The other half of that well-known duet, **needs** and **interests**. The phrase rightly suggests that pupils are to be considered as customers or clients; it protests against their being treated as receptacles, or little animals to be trained, shaped or moulded. Some writers, also quite rightly, have been quick to point up the possible *naïveté* of such an appeal. 'I need x' means 'I haven't got it and ought to have it'; in other words there is a built-in value-judgement in the **concept**. A child's **needs** are in effect those things he ought to have in order to grow into a fully developed human being. What that is is another question! No amount of psychological research into hierarchies of **needs**, drive-reduction, etc., will establish what a child's **educational needs** are unless this question is first tackled.

For a psychological account *see,* e.g. DENNIS CHILD, *Psychology and the Teacher,* ch. 3, pp. 35ff. (Holt, Rinehart & Winston, New York, 1973). For a development of the critique outlined above *see* R. F. DEARDEN, *The Philosophy of Primary Education,* ch. 2 (Routledge & Kegan Paul, London, 1968).

Numeracy
One of the 'four aces' (literacy, **numeracy, oracy, graphicacy**), it is referred to in the Crowther Report (HMSO, 1959, paras. 401ff.) as the ability 'to think quantitatively, to realise how far our problems are ones of degree even when they appear as problems of kind'. *See* **graphicacy**.

Objectives
Insistence upon specifying the **objectives** of a lesson or course has become widespread in teacher training, on in-service courses, in schools where rethinking of the **curriculum** takes place. What is being asked is usually:

(i) that the pupil becomes the subject of the verb; what will the *pupil* have achieved at the end of the lesson, by half term, etc?
(ii) that the teacher thinks less of the **content** of what he teaches, more of what the learner will be able to *do*; for instance, he will be able to explain the differences between communism and fascism,

or solve a quadratic equation—the emphasis being on the verb in each case;

(iii) that this be specified as clearly as possible; for instance, 'locate a book in a library' is better than 'use a library', 'name principal features of . . .' than 'understand . . . .'

This sounds simple enough, but much ink has been spilled over it. Perhaps it will serve here to list a few obvious advantages and disadvantages in specifying objectives.

Advantages

(a) It concentrates attention on the pupils rather than on teachers.
(b) It puts the screw on those who muddle through, or who are not sure what they are trying to do.
(c) It makes it easier to check results—**evaluation** (curriculum design).

Disadvantages

(a) It may result in concentration on the trivial—on facts and low level learning.
(b) Taken to extremes it can become absurd—the list of **objectives** can be enormous and unmanageable.
(c) It tends to be linked with a doctrine that all learning consists in changes in **behaviour** (*see* **behavioural objectives**).
(d) We often do not want to specify in advance *exactly* what a pupil will do, say, as a result of reading a poem.

There appears to be some reaction, therefore, against the **objectives model** among the pundits; the author's view is that there is far more to be gained from trying to pin down one's **objectives** than from rejecting this approach, powerful though the objections to it are. *See* also **principles of procedure.**

DENIS LAWTON, *Social Change, Educational Theory and Curriculum Planning,* ch. 1 (University of London Press, London, 1973).

Objective testing

'Objective' in this sense means that the marker's subjective judgement is not involved; the answer is correct or incorrect. Most teachers know about 'blank-filling' or multiple-choice tests, though the art of writing them is not so well appreciated. There is considerable skill, for instance, in choosing 'distractors', the incorrect answers in multiple-choice items which nevertheless look plausible enough to tempt the guessers. Two points are, perhaps, worth emphasising.

1. Objective tests need not be confined to facts; they can be used to test for quite high levels of understanding. For example **(analysis)**:

    Following the playing of a piece of music the student is asked to state whether the general structure of the composition is
    (a) Theme and variations
    (b) Theme; development; restatement
    (c) Theme; development; Theme 2; development
    (d) Introduction; theme; development. (Bloom, **Taxonomy**, p. 161)

2. Well written objective tests take a lot of time and care to devise, but once prepared they can be marked extremely rapidly. Thus, in cases where such a test can be as effective as, say, an essay-type examination in the **evaluation** (curriculum design) of one's **objectives**, they have a distinct advantage, often at a time when teachers are under some pressure to publish results; probably more important, however, they can give rapid **feedback** to the pupils.

BARRIE HUDSON (ed.), *Assessment Techniques* (Methuen, London, 1973).

Operational terms (*See* also **principles of procedure**)
Objectives, according to Robert Mager and others, should be written in **operational terms.** This means much the same as **behavioural** in practice, the difference being, perhaps, that the former only implies that such **objectives** are workable, manageable, whereas the latter carries with it the additional implication that they are concerned with visible and measurable **behaviour.** It may be that the difference, if such it is, is worth pursuing; are workable **objectives** possible which are not **behavioural**?

R. F. MAGER, *Preparing Instructional Objectives* (Fearon, Belmont, Calif., 1962).

Oracy (*See* **graphicacy**)
The ability to speak coherently, as opposed to literacy, the ability to handle the written word. The origin of the term is unclear, but it forms part of a quite interesting classification of **aims** which might be termed 'the four aces'.

Organisation
According to Wheeler and others, one of the essential stages in the **rational curriculum plan** *(see also* **model**). When **content** and **learning experiences** have been decided, you then need to assemble them; this is the stage of **organisation**, possibly also of **integration**. The pieces have to be fitted together, rather like a jigsaw puzzle, except that they can be assembled in many different ways; perhaps a mosaic would be a

better analogy. The example below shows how such a collection of topics and activities can be put together. **Scope, logical sequence, continuity, integration, vertical** and **horizontal relationships** have all been built in, so that the whole has a distinct **structure**. *See* also **organising centres.**

Scheme of work for one term—class project — Age 10–11

Continuity—Sequence—Vertical Relationships	Science	Art	Language/R.E.
Unit 4	The digestive system—where does the food go?	Form, colour and texture. Theme: food, fruits of the earth (collage)	The world's food. Poverty and famine—Oxfam materials
Unit 3	Respiratory and circulatory systems Visit of District Nurse	Form and colour: man out of his element—climbers, divers (silhouettes)	Life and breath. Writing—divers, astronauts. The ascent of Everest
Unit 2	Muscles and tissues. Movement: experiments with weights	Form—in action. 'Action Man'—walking, running (strip cartoons)	Learning to move. Infancy to old age—seven ages of man
Unit 1	The skeleton: bones and their functions	Form—static. Skulls and skeletons (frieze)	Story: 'Valley of Dry Bones'. Writing—skeletons (*Carnival of the Animals*)

BEGIN HERE

Integration—Scope—Horizontal Relationships

Organising centres

The topics, the themes, which form the outline of a course; the main beads on the string. Usually they are not much more than slabs of **content**: Wordsworth this term, *Othello* next. But it could be important, for instance, whether one chose either:

A. Unit 1 Communications: 1774, 1874, 1974
Unit 2 Occupation/industry: 1774, 1874, 1974
Unit 3 Social/family life: 1774, 1874, 1974

or

B. Unit 1 The 18th century: Communications, occupations, social
　　　history, etc.

The **content** might be the same, but the **organising centres** are
different—suggesting different **objectives**?

D. K. WHEELER, *Curriculum Process,* pp. 249ff. (University of London Press,
London, 1967).

Organising principle *See* **taxonomy**

Overarching aim
One occasionally meets this term in the literature. Is there perhaps
some way in which the **aim** of education could be neatly expressed, a
sort of 'umbrella' **aim** under which all other educational **aims** could
shelter or be 'subsumed'? Hence the metaphor of the arch.

Harris claims that **autonomy** constitutes such an **aim**. 'Can you
think' he writes, 'of any plausible educational **aim** which would be
inconsistent with the promotion of personal **autonomy**? If so,
which—and why? If not, why not?' Good question.

ALAN HARRIS, *Open University Course E 283,* Unit 8.

P

Paradigm
A framework, pattern of thinking, which we take for granted. The
scientific **paradigm** controls many of our basic assumptions—we
assume for instance that, say, 'achievement = intelligence +
motivation'; all these can be measured, and research will tell us what is
possible.

However, according to some writers in **sociology of the curriculum,** there is a quite different way of seeing the same situation—a **phenomenological paradigm.** Intelligence does not make us what we are; we create our own world. The teacher's job is to respect this, to work with it; act as consultant, not instructor, respond rather than manipulate.

Rational curriculum planning works within a **'positivist'** paradigm which assumes that man can take a detached view of the situation in which he finds himself and can thus see it objectively, act on it and control it; and is thus out of sympathy with the view outlined in the paragraph above.

Open University Course E 282, Unit 5, 'Pedagogy and the Teacher's presentation of Self' (Geoffrey Esland).

Parameter
Though having a precise definition in mathematics, this term is used loosely in **curriculum** literature as a scale, dimension or specification; for instance, when planning a course in literature, one would need to have certain **parameters** in mind, such as the breadth and depth of the treatment, either of which could be varied relative to the other.

Pattern
One of the **criteria** of **learning experiences,** referring not so much to the quality of the experiences or activities in themselves, as to the way they are assembled and linked. Wheeler, in **Curriculum Process,** subdivides this category into:

(i) balance—for example between activities designed to achieve **cognitive, affective** and **psychomotor objectives**—how much play-reading, how much improvised drama, for instance?
(ii) **continuity**—both in terms of **organisation** of the course, and also in terms of the timetable, avoiding, for example, what have been called 'squads' working in 'spasms', punctuated by bells.

D.K. WHEELER, *Curriculum Process,* pp. 158–68, (University of London Press, London, 1967).

Phenomenology
This alarming word 'denotes a particular orientation to the study of man—one which is concerned with his subjective ordering of experience', in other words, we all see the world in a different way. Writers on the **sociology of the curriculum** ask us to look at what really happens (the phenomena). What determines, say, the grammar school **curriculum**? Answer: a certain **ideology.** What makes some

favour a subject **curriculum**, others an activity **curriculum**? Answer: their social background, etc. *See also* **Paradigm**.

Open University Course E 282, passim (esp. Unit 5, 11–4).

Positivist view (of curriculum) (*See* **sociology of the curriculum**)
That 'common sense' view (within the **positivist paradigm**) which has as a basic assumption that man is a rational creature who can make plans and put them into practice. It is usually contrasted with a **phenomenological** view which seems rather more sceptical.

Power (Bruner) (*See* **structure**)

Principle learning
The American psychologist, Robert Gagné (see **conditions of learning**) makes a distinction between the learning of **concepts** and **principles**; he cites the **principle** 'work = force × distance'. To demonstrate this **principle** the pupil must identify not one, but several **concepts** and their proper sequence. One could say a **principle** is a relationship between two or more **concepts**.

Two points: (a) This looks to the writer like levels 2 and 4 of Part 1 of Bloom's **Taxonomy**; (b) The distinction is sometimes difficult to maintain, for instance, 'weight' is a **concept**, 'mass' a **principle**. Or are they?

ROBERT GAGNÉ, 'The Learning of Principles' in E. STONES (ed.), *Readings in Educational Psychology*, p. 67ff. (Methuen, London, 1970).

Principles of procedure
Specifying **objectives** is often taken to be the most important feature of the **rational curriculum plan**. Yet there is strong opposition on a number of counts, one of the main ones being that it is frequently (not necessarily always) mistaken to specify in advance exactly what a pupil is to learn.

But what might replace **objectives**? One answer suggested is **principles of procedure**. For example, to say that a pupil will précis a passage is not, by this account, an **objective**, certainly not a **behavioural** one; but the teacher, and one hopes the pupil, knows what constitutes a good précis, and the teacher can **evaluate** it according to whether it is, say, comprehensive, accurate and elegant. These are **criteria** or **principles**.

To the author it does not seem crucial whether one calls these **principles** or **objectives**; the point being made is surely unexceptionable, i.e. detailed prespecification in **behavioural** terms may not be called for.

Open University Course E 283, Unit 7 (Richard Pring); or the same author's 'Curriculum Courses: an Interdisciplinary Failure' in P. H. TAYLOR & JACK WALTON, *The Curriculum: Research, Innovation and Change*, p. 68ff. (Ward Lock, London, 1973).

Problem centred curriculum
One of the basic **curriculum** types (*see* **activity, broad fields, core, subject-based**). The focus of study is a problem which needs contributions from a number of subjects to treat it adequately, perhaps in an **interdisciplinary enquiry** approach. It can perhaps be distinguished from the **core** type in that no one subject forms the central thread.

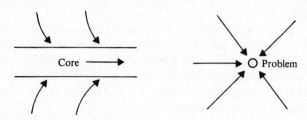

An example might be the Schools Council Humanities Project, where the central problems are open, controversial ones such as Poverty, the Family, Education.

Programmed learning
In **programmed learning**, or better, programmed instruction, the **content** or skill to be learned is defined and analysed; presented in a carefully prearranged sequence; at each step the learner responds, makes a choice, thus checking that he is following the instruction; and, finally, he receives immediate **feedback**, works at his own pace and checks his own progress. This can be done by means of a teaching machine or a programmed text. The **programmed learning** movement, popular in the early 1960's, has now found its place in the wider world of educational **technology**.

For a programmed text, *see* R. F. MAGER, *Preparing Instructional Objectives* (Fearon, Belmont, Calif., 1962). For a readable account of programmed learning, *see* W. K. RICHMOND, *Teachers and Machines* (Methuen, London, 1965).

Psychological sequence
Sometimes contrasted with **logical sequence**, something as follows: the **logical** structure of a subject is very different from the way it was

discovered, and hence the way a child should learn. For instance, so the argument goes, the **logical** way to teach reading is to take the alphabet first, then use it to make words; but this is not the natural way, as we meet and recognise words long before we learn all the letters.

But the contrast is false, and stems from assuming that **logical** means deductive, and that step B (e.g. irregular verbs) cannot be undertaken until step A (regular verbs) has been mastered. Induction, deriving rules from instances, is just as **logical**: to borrow a term from **programmed learning**, *Egrule* (example leading to rule) is just as respectable as *Ruleg* (the opposite). *See also* **learnability**.

R. F. DEARDEN, *The Philosophy of Primary Education*, ch. 6 (Routledge & Kegan Paul, London, 1968).

Psychomotor objectives
Objectives in the **psychomotor domain** have to do with the learning of physical skills. Bloom and his team have not yet produced a classification of this field, but one or two outline versions have appeared. *See* **taxonomy**.

R

Rational curriculum plan
This is a shorthand phrase used to describe the view that a systematic strategy for **curriculum** planning is both possible and desirable. It usually, though not always, refers to the so-called **objectives model (objectives, content, learning experiences, evaluation)** or some similar design sequence, and is even coming to be known as R.C.P. for short. It does not necessarily entail a **behavioural** view of **objectives**, but it does seem to involve a **positivist** belief that innovation and change can be planned for. It may be contrasted with the current view **(sociology**

of the curriculum) that knowledge is best seen as 'property' or as a 'social construction', and that social forces and **ideologies** largely determine the form the **curriculum** takes.

Realms of meaning

Philip Phenix's book of this name is a seminal work. Its sub-title is 'A Philosophy of the Curriculum for General Education'. Any teacher looking for a searching yet readable account of the **logic** of his subject need look no further. The argument goes broadly as follows:

1. Human beings are creatures who have the power to experience meanings.
2. General education is the process of engendering essential meanings.
3. There are six fundamental patterns of meaning, related to distinctive modes of human understanding. They are:

1. **Symbolics** (mathematics, language)	2. **Empirics** (the sciences)	3. **Esthetics** (the arts)
4. **Ethics** (morality)	5. **Synnoetics** (personal knowledge)	6. **Synoptics** (history, religion and philosophy)

4. The **curriculum** must, to be balanced, include '**representative ideas**' from these **realms of meaning**, since they 'embrace the basic competences that general education should develop in every person'.

It is interesting to compare the sort of balance suggested with that of the standard British secondary **curriculum**; Whitfield has done this in *Disciplines of the Curriculum*, which is also quite a useful introduction to Phenix's ideas.

P. H. PHENIX, *Realms of Meaning* (McGraw-Hill, Maidenhead, 1964).

R. C. WHITFIELD (ed.), *Disciplines of the Curriculum* (McGraw-Hill, Maidenhead, 1971).

Recall *See* **knowledge** (Bloom)

Receiving *See* **attending**

Reception learning *See* **meaningful learning**

Reinforcement
Positive and negative **reinforcement**, often loosely referred to as reward and punishment, are basic ingredients of learning theory. Success is its own reward; successful learning needs little more than **feedback** to be reinforced. The link with **curriculum** planning is in the area of **evaluation** and **feedback**. Any teacher knows the value and power of praise, encouragement, even criticism as a means of **motivation**. What is less clear is the best form and pacing of such **reinforcement**, as an aid to teaching. At what point does one say, 'good, now try to follow through more' or 'now can you express that in a formula?' The right remark at the right time is often virtually accidental; the skilful teacher is perhaps the one who can spot the critical moment and make the remark that enables the pupil to say 'oh, I see'.

JEROME BRUNER, *Toward a Theory of Instruction,* pp. 50–3, 68ff. (Harvard University Press, Cambridge, Mass., 1968).

Reiteration
An aspect of **sequence** in the **organisation** stage of **curriculum process. Key concepts** often need to be repeated, illustrated and explained in different ways to ensure they 'take'. This is the main function of practice; further examples should be the same, only different, as it were.

Relevance
One of the **criteria** to be applied to **learning experiences**; wherever possible these should be **'relevant to life'.** What exactly **'relevant'** means is perhaps not crystal clear; certainly it is not simply to be equated with vocational. But the **curriculum** should have something to do with real life. 'Teachers', says Wheeler, 'may sometimes succeed in living in ivory towers, students (pupils) never'.

D. K. WHEELER, *Curriculum Process,* pp. 168–70 (University of London Press, London, 1967).

Reliability
One of the **criteria** of any good **evaluation** instrument or test. In a **reliable** examination two pupils who do equally well get the same mark. This may sound obvious, but it is not always so. Subjective **evaluation** may be unreliable, though it need not be. Many teachers

must know the feeling of having marked a very similar composition twenty scripts back, and wondering what grade they awarded!

How to prevent unreliability? Experience helps, but a clear set of **objectives** or **criteria** is a much better guarantee. **Objective tests** ought to be highly **reliable**; if they are unsuitable, such devices as multiple impression marking, moderating of samples etc., can be used. The story of the Chief Examiner who wrote a model answer, which he mislaid, and which was found and failed by one of the other examiners may be apocryphal, but it illustrates the need for reliable **evaluation.**

Representation *See* **structure** (also **enactive, iconic, symbolic representation**)

Representative ideas
Not unlike **basic themes**, but the actual phrase is one of Philip Phenix (*see* **Realms of Meaning**). 'The only effective solution to the surfeit of **knowledge**' he says, 'is a drastic process of simplification. This **aim** can be achieved by discovering for each **discipline** those seminal or **key ideas** that provide clues to the entire **discipline**' (p. 11). He cites, in biology, natural selection, organism; in literature, metaphor, myth; in language, phoneme, morpheme.

In each **discipline** there are hierarchies of these ideas worked out by specialists; Phenix emphasises that the **curriculum** should exemplify them, not teach them explicitly; they are for teachers, not pupils. Quoting Whitehead, he says 'the problem of education is to make the pupil see the wood by means of the trees'.

P. H. PHENIX, *Realms of Meaning,* ch. 26 (McGraw-Hill, Maidenhead, 1964).

Resources, Resource-based learning
The term has links with a whole network of current 'progressive' ideas (e.g. **integration, systems analysis, team-teaching**). Its slogan might be 'source books, not course books', but **resources** include teachers, **technology** (hardware), as well as books and other materials (software). With a shortage of specialist teachers efficient use of **resources** is important, but there is also an underlying **ideology**—teacher as consultant rather than class instructor.

L. C. TAYLOR, *Resources for Learning* (Penguin, Harmondsworth, 1971).

Responding
The second level of the **affective domain** of Bloom's **Taxonomy**. At this level the pupil's **attitude** to a subject is one where he begins to

give, rather than just take. He is interested, likes answering questions, he may carry on with work spontaneously after the lesson. He does not yet **value** the subject (level 3), but is 'sufficiently committed . . . that he will seek it out and gain satisfaction from engaging in it'.

Rote learning *See* **meaningful learning**

Routinisation
A possible **organising principle** for the **psychomotor domain** of the **Taxonomy.**

S

Scope
Scope and **sequence** are the two main dimensions of the **organisation** stage of **curriculum process. Scope** refers to **horizontal relationships, sequence** to the **vertical.** Wheeler gives examples of 'scope and **sequence** charts' from some American **core curricula,** which seem not unlike some of our secondary non-examination courses. For a simple primary school example *see* **organisation.**

D.K. WHEELER, *Curriculum Process,* pp. 247–8 (University of London Press, London, 1967).

Sequence (*See also* **logical, psychological sequence**)
This has to do with **vertical relationships** at the **organisation** stage of **curriculum process.** It means arranging the subject in a suitable order for the most effective learning. There do not appear to be any fixed rules beyond a few fairly obvious general principles, such as:

   (i) simpler should precede more complex;
  (ii) concrete should lead to abstract;
 (iii) easy should anticipate difficult;
 (iv) plan for **reiteration** of **key concepts,** etc.

Bruner's notion of a **spiral curriculum** is worth following up in this respect: one 'comes round' to a **basic theme** at a later stage in a different context and at a higher level.

D. K. WHEELER, *Curriculum Process*, p. 246ff. (University of London Press, London, 1967).

Significance

One of the **criteria** to bear in mind when choosing **content.** Other things being equal, we should go for what is of central importance, **representative ideas,** fundamental or **key concepts**; facts can then be selected to illustrate them. Our lessons on the Vikings may be interesting, well prepared and adapted to our pupils' abilities, but have we time for them any more? Is there room for a project on the Great Barrier Reef?

D.K. WHEELER, *Curriculum Process,* p. 220 (University of London Press, London, 1967).

Simulation

Closely associated with **gaming**, the essence of **simulation** is pretending. A pupil may act out the part, say, of a parent in a role-play situation; the other well-known type is the 'in-tray' exercise, where, say, the problems facing the senior management staff of a developing comprehensive school are cast in the form of letters, memoranda, notes appearing in the Head's in-tray, and discussion is invited on the best course of action.

WILLIAM TAYLOR, *Heading for Change* (Routledge & Kegan Paul, London, 1973).

Sociology (of the curriculum)

Sociology of education used to be concerned with such matters as the effect of social background on educability, or the way in which the educational system sorts out the sheep and the goats. Now the sociologists have shifted their attention to **knowledge** and the **curriculum. Knowledge** can be seen as 'property', for example, Latin and Shakespeare are a sort of passport to respectability, which secondary modern pupils do not need. This is a **phenomenological**, as opposed to the traditional **positivist** view of the **curriculum.**

Some controversy currently rages over what exactly is being said. Is this *the* way of explaining present **curricula,** or just another, useful and thought-provoking way? Perhaps the best jobs *have* tended to go to those who studied Latin, but is this the *only* reason why some schools are reluctant to abandon the Classics? Do traditional subject divisions *only* reflect and perpetuate power groups and systems of control? The battle continues.

M. F. D. YOUNG, *Knowledge and Control* (Collier-Macmillan, New York and London, 1971).
Education for Teaching, Autumn 1972 (articles by Gorbutt, Pring).

Spiral curriculum

Another idea from Jerome Bruner. He writes: 'if one respects the ways of thought of the growing child . . . it is possible to introduce him at an early age to the ideas and styles that in later life make an educated man'. Why then a spiral? The pupil returns to familiar ideas

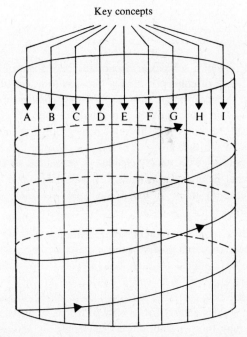

and **concepts**, but presented through **alternative samples**, and at a higher level. Thus **concepts** do not have to be unlearned. An obvious example would be sex education; no stories about storks please—unless they are obviously stories. A truthful, but simple and partial account is needed in the early years, which can be the basis of a more complete understanding later on, when we 'come round' to it again.

JEROME BRUNER, *The Process of Education,* pp. 52–4 (Harvard University Press, Cambridge, Mass., 1960).

Stimulus

Though presumably having roots in **stimulus**-response theories of learning and conditioning (*see* **behavioural objectives**), in the field of **curriculum** this word often refers to the initial 'starter-session' in a **team-teaching** situation; it can be a **lead lesson**, a film, a speaker, a visit, etc.

Such a **stimulus** requires **follow up**, and perhaps secondary stimulation in the form of displays of work, etc.

DAVID WARWICK, *Team Teaching* (University of London Press, London, 1971).

Structure

There seem to be two distinct ways in which this word is used in the field of **curriculum**:

(a) The **structure** of a subject or **discipline**. Each **form of knowledge** has a network of **concepts**, largely peculiar to it; for instance, the ideas of 'grace' and 'sin' are closely linked in religious thinking—you can't properly understand one if you do not understand the other. It is the 'logical geography' of the **discipline**. (*See* **logic of subject**.)

(b) The orderliness with which an idea is presented to the learner. This is what Bruner often means; the way the teacher 'structures' the material to make it comprehensible. He may do it, says Bruner, by:

   (i) **enactive, iconic** or **symbolic representation**, skilfully used;

   (ii) the **economy** and **power** of the explanation. For instance, 'it is more economical (though less powerful) to summarise the American Civil War as "a battle over slavery" than as "a struggle between an expanding industrial region and one built upon a class society for control of federal economic policy" '. One may have to choose between **economy** and **power** (as in compiling this book) yet some very powerful ideas have been expressed with great economy, as, say, in 'the world's shortest poem'—

<blockquote>
How odd
of God
To choose
The Jews.
</blockquote>

(W. N. Ewer)

Subject-based curriculum
This needs little explanation; it is the traditional **curriculum** with which most secondary teachers are familiar. It goes with specialist teachers, and a strong sense of the need to preserve the **disciplines** and their standards.

It is under some pressure from the claims of other types—*see* **activity, broad fields, core,** and **problem-centred curricula.**

Suitability
An everyday word, included here because it appears in lists of **criteria** for **learning experiences.** These should be suitable to the pupil's mental ability, his stage of **cognitive** development. By and large, the primary school child is at the **concrete operational** stage, and cannot handle abstract **concepts.** But this is only a generalisation; some young children are able, say, to cope with formulae remarkably early, some adults are still at sea when faced with quite simple **formal concepts.**

D. K. WHEELER, *Curriculum Process,* pp. 154–7 (University of London Press, London, 1967).

Summative evaluation
Evaluation, such as the traditional examination, which takes place at the end of a course or project, which 'sums up'. It has been fashionable to play down this form of **evaluation;** formative **evaluation,** the argument runs, is much more important; what is needed is, say, course work assessment, continuous **feedback.**

But the argument for summative evaluation needs to be stated particularly when courses, as opposed to pupils, are being considered; not all **curriculum** plans, innovations, schemes will be successful. When teachers put a lot of work into devising new courses, it is hard to admit failure, yet sometimes it is necessary to stand back and say 'no more modifications, no more attempts at improvement; let's start again'.

S. WISEMAN & D. PIDGEON, *Curriculum Evaluation* (N.F.E.R., Slough, 1972).

Syllabus
A list of the **content** of a course. The word simply means 'collection'.

Symbolic representation
Bruner's third level of representation, the process by which we 'translate experience into a **model** of the world'. It is thinking in words or language. Whereas **enactive** representation is thinking 'through the

seat of one's pants' and **iconic** representation thinking in mental pictures or images, this level uses symbols, words, language, which increase the power of thinking in countless ways. A lot of meaning is squashed into '$E = Mc^2$' or 'gather ye rosebuds while ye may'.

JEROME BRUNER, *Toward a Theory of Instruction*, p. 11 (Harvard University Press, Cambridge, Mass., 1966).

Symbolics

The first of Phenix's **Realms of Meaning.** This comprises ordinary language, mathematics and 'non-discursive symbolic forms'. Ordinary language is concerned with formal conventions 'created in the laboratory of culture', e.g. French 'et' and English 'and' do the same job. Mathematics is the language of complete abstraction, concerned not primarily with the real world, but with the formal world of pure symbolic form. Non-discursive symbolic forms constitute a third type of symbolism. They are used to express feelings and insights. They do not have to make any sort of consecutive sense; this is the language of poetry, drama and myth.

P.H. PHENIX, *Realms of Meaning,* ch. 5–7 (McGraw-Hill, Maidenhead, 1964).

Synnoetics

One of Phenix's **Realms of Meaning. Synnoetics** is the term he uses for personal knowledge; it 'refers to meanings in which a person has direct insight into other beings (or oneself)'. It is existential—Phenix refers to the 'I-thou relation' notion found in the writing of Martin Buber, and also to Freudian psycho-analytic theory. In the school **curriculum** the development of this sort of insight would probably be most likely to find a place among the **objectives** of history, literature and moral education.

P. H. PHENIX, *Realms of Meaning,* ch. 16 (McGraw-Hill, Maidenhead, 1964).

Synoptics

The last of Phenix's **Realms of Meaning, synoptics** means seeing things together, as a whole, and meanings in this realm have 'an integrative function, uniting meanings from all the realms (**symbolics, empirics, esthetics, ethics, synnoetics**) into a unified perspective, i.e. providing a "single vision" or "synopsis" of meanings'.

It comprises the **disciplines** of history, religion and philosophy; according to Phenix, 'historical understanding is personal insight expressed in ordinary language, informed by scientific **knowledge,** transformed by **esthetic** imagination and infused by moral consciousness'. Where history deals with events in time, religion is concerned with the ultimate. Philosophy 'is not even limited, as history and religion are, to certain dimensions of experience, such as the past or the ultimate. All dimensions of all kinds of experience come within its purview'.

P. H. PHENIX, *Realms of Meaning,* ch. 18–20 (McGraw-Hill, Maidenhead, 1964).

Synthesis

The fifth level of the **cognitive domain** of Bloom's **Taxonomy.** It is defined as 'the putting together of elements and parts so as to form a whole', in a 'unique communication'. For example, a pupil who has grasped the idea of the expansion of metals, and also the concept of an electrical circuit, and combines the two to suggest, say, a means of triggering off a signal when the expansion of railway lines means a risk of buckled tracks, has done some **synthesis** of a simple kind. It does not seem necessarily to involve learning at a high academic level.

Systems analysis

This is an almost impossibly difficult approach to **curriculum** planning to explain briefly. Here is a very crude attempt:

1. A computer can be programmed to produce a result or a solution to a problem, provided that:
   (a) all the information needed is fed in;
   (b) it is in a precise language which the computer can interpret.
2. In principle, it is claimed, a similar process can be carried out in **curriculum** planning, provided that:
   (a) all **key concepts** are defined;
   (b) the outcomes desired are specified;
   (c) all the necessary information, constraints, etc., are fed in.
3. The whole can be expressed mathematically, or in the form of **flow charts, critical paths,** alternative solutions, etc.

However, the problems are enormous; practically none of the requirements can be met; and the whole smacks, perhaps, of a master plan which teachers are employed to carry out. Is this what education is about?

R. G. CAVE, *An Introduction to Curriculum Development,* ch. 5 (Ward Lock, London, 1971).

T

Taxonomy

The word basically means 'classification' as used, for instance, in natural history. Part 1 of Bloom's *Taxonomy of Educational*

*A tentative relationship between cognitive,
affective and psychomotor objectives*

Domain	COGNITIVE (Bloom)	AFFECTIVE (Krathwohl)	PSYCHOMOTOR (Alles)
Organising Principle	COMPLEXITY of mental operations	INTERNALISA–TION of values/attitudes	ROUTINISATION of skills
'High level' activities	6 Evaluation 5 Synthesis 4 Analysis	5 Characterisation by value-complex 4 Organisation	3 Routine level (speed, elegance, semi-automatic routine inc. *adaptive* skills)
Common to this level are activities where the learner's behaviour becomes, as well as autonomous, complex, conceptually interlocking and adaptive. Overlap between the cognitive and affective particularly obvious here?			
'Middle level' activities	3 Application 2 Comprehension	3 Valuing 2 Responding	2 Pre-routine level (more confident, needs less help inc. *some* adaptive skills)
Common to this level are activities where the learner begins to be *autonomous* and can *transfer* knowledge, attitudes and skills to similar or *new* situations. His learning becomes his own: active, individual, giving as well as taking.			
'Low level' activities	1 Knowledge (recall)	1 Receiving (attending)	1 Initiatory level (hesitant, needs help)
Common to this level are activities in which the learner's behaviour is limited, inflexible, unimaginative. He 'takes' rather than gives, is passive rather than active. He does not do much for himself.			

Objectives was published in 1956. It dealt with **objectives** in the **cognitive domain**, that is the area of **knowledge** and understanding. Part 2, 'The **Affective Domain**', (**attitudes**, values) followed in 1964, its principal editor being D. R. Krathwohl. Each volume was the result of an impressive amount of research and consultation with American educationists and teachers. Part 3, dealing with the **psychomotor domain** (physical skills) has not been published, though the author has come across an interesting outline **taxonomy** in this area by Jinapala Alles.

The argument is briefly this: low level **cognitive objectives** are concerned with the minimum of understanding or mental manipulation, whereas at the highest level we have the maximum of understanding, the ability to handle, arrange and judge the force of a number of ideas and arguments; the **organising principle** is **complexity** of mental operations. In the **affective domain** the **organising principle** is one of **internalisation:** at the lowest level we find the minimum of involvement and commitment, at the highest level the values and **attitudes** concerned permeate the subject's character and personality. In Alles' version of the **psychomotor domain,** the learning of skills at the lowest level is characterised by hesitant, clumsy and slow performance; at the highest level the skill is performed with speed, elegance and flexibility. **The organising principle** is **routinisation**.

A possible relationship between the **objectives** in the three **domains** is set out below: at the bottom we have the beginner, dependent on **recall**, diffident, passive, uninvolved. At the top is the 'man of parts', coherent, committed, confident and skilful—the educated man himself!

B. S. BLOOM (ed.), *Taxonomy of educational objectives: the classification of educational goals.* Handbook I: 'Cognitive Domain', 1956; Handbook II: 'Affective Domain', 1964 (David McKay Co., New York). Condensed versions of these can be found in R. HOOPER (ed.), *The Curriculum: Context, Design and Development* (Oliver & Boyd, Edinburgh, for Open University, 1971).

Team Teaching (*See also* **blocked timetable)**
Basic ingredients: a large number of pupils, say a year group; the teachers available; rooms, equipment, materials; the willingness to plan together, using all these **resources** to the best advantage, without any prior assumptions about size of groups. It has been called 'an economic and fairly democratic way of organising a school'. (It can also become an **ideology**, but that's another story!) It tends to include **lead lessons** or **stimulus** sessions; **follow up** work in groups of various sizes, and displays or exhibitions to co-ordinate the work. It is likely to lead to **integration** or **interdisciplinary enquiry**.

Its advantages: a more efficient use of manpower and equipment; group size adjustable to the activity concerned; a good system in which to train students and probationers; a framework in which more fundamental changes may be tried out. Disadvantages: threat to teachers' **autonomy**; problems if the teachers in the team are anti-pathetic; or do not pull their weight; possible problems of control ('isn't John in your group?').

DAVID WARWICK, *Team Teaching* (University of London Press, London, 1971).

Technology, educational

Teaching, it has been argued, is still in the age of craftmanship, in a world otherwise dominated by **technology**. Mechanical aids ('hardware') are still suspect in many schools. **Programmed learning** appeared on the scene in the early 1960's and was hailed by many as a breakthrough; but it was gradually seen to be part of a larger whole, which included computer-assisted instruction, the management of **resources**, characteristics of media, **systems analysis**, etc. The subject tends now to be treated within the same framework as the **rational curriculum plan**, i.e. **objectives**, methods, **resources, evaluation**.

W. K. RICHMOND, *Teachers and Machines* (1965), esp. ch. 1, and *The Concept of Educational Technology* (1970) Methuen, London.

Theory

Words! Words! Words! The term **curriculum theory** is almost em-barrassing; to some it is moribund. **Curriculum** design, development, planning are fairly respectable; **theory** is rather a dirty word.

One view is that, following the **paradigm** of science, a **theory** of the **curriculum** would include the formation and testing of hypotheses, and ultimately the production of generalisations and laws which would explain and predict. No such **theory** exists.

Others prefer Hirst's concept of a 'practical **theory**' guiding and informing practice, the sort of prescriptive **theory** of which Kerr's **model** is an outline. This, too, hardly constitutes a **theory** proper, even of a non-scientific kind; but it is theoretical, and does provide a strategy for planning.

D. J. O'CONNOR & P. H. HIRST, 'The Nature and Scope of Educational Theory', in *New Essays in the Philosophy of Education* (Routledge & Kegan Paul, London, 1973).
Open University Course E 283, Unit 6, 'The Current Debate'.

U

Utility
One of the criteria for **content** selection. **Content**, as well as being **significant, authentic** and so on, may also come in useful in one's job or help one to pass an examination! Fair enough; few Heads would think it wise, or even right, to ignore these demands on the **curriculum.** 'Other things being equal' says Wheeler (p. 224) 'that selection of subject matter should be selected which is most useful to the learner in solving his problems now and in the future'. But only 'other things being equal'!

D. K. WHEELER, *Curriculum Process,* p. 223 (University of London Press, London, 1967).

V

Validity
An important **criterion** of **content, learning experiences** and **evaluation.** The meaning is essentially the same in all cases, that of being related to the **objectives.** Thus, if our **objective** is that a pupil will be able to describe and explain orally the climate of the British Isles, then the rain cycle will be **valid content**, oral question and answer a **valid learning experience**, and an oral test a **valid** way of **evaluating** it. A collection of weather lore rhymes, a project based on library research, and a written test may be valuable, but they will probably not be **valid** for the named **objective.**

D. K. WHEELER, *Curriculum Process,* pp. 147, 218, 273 (University of London Press, London, 1967).

Value complex

Characterisation by a **value complex** is the highest level of the **affective domain** of Bloom's **Taxonomy**. It represents the peak of the **internalisation** process. A person who meets this level of **objectives**, say in regard to geography, sees the world as a geographer, over a period of time. A love of geography is part of his character.

Valuing

Level 3 of the **affective domain** of Bloom's **Taxonomy. Behaviour** at this level 'is motivated, not by the desire to comply or obey, but by the individual's commitment to the underlying **value** guiding the **behaviour**'. So if young Jane turns up at school with bits of Roman pottery she found on holiday and asks for history, choosing it as her particular contribution to a class project, she is probably working at this level.

Variety

An obvious **criterion** to bear in mind when selecting **learning experiences**; pupils learn at different rates, in different ways. **Variety** is important not simply to allay boredom, but so that pupils can find the sort of experience or explanation they need. A useful exercise is to list as many different learning activities as you can think of which can take place in a classroom (the list is not endless, but it is quite long); then use more than you do at present!

D. K. WHEELER, *Curriculum Process,* p. 151–4 (University of London Press, London, 1967).

Verification procedures *See* forms of knowledge

Vertical relationships

This term refers to relationships of **continuity** and **sequence** in the **organisation** of **content** and **learning experiences**. Thus what is learned in mathematics in the first year will be related to what follows in the second year, and so on. To attempt to ensure such **continuity**, particularly in building on work done in previous years, many schools like to arrange for the same teacher to stay with a class over two or more years.

Z

Zetetics

This had to be included if only because it begins with 'Z'. Zetetics, according to Professor Tykociner of the University of Illinois in a remarkable article written in 1964, is the study of the origin of systematised knowledge. Its aim is to produce an ordered classification of human knowledge. In this fascinating paper is to be found a compendious map, a simplified version of which is given below, without further comment. The reader may make of it what he will.

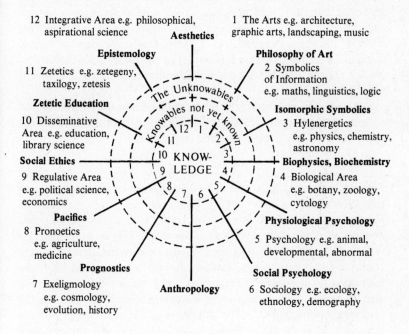

12 Integrative Area e.g. philosophical, aspirational science

Aesthetics

1 The Arts e.g. architecture, graphic arts, landscaping, music

Epistemology

11 Zetetics e.g. zetegeny, taxilogy, zetesis

Philosophy of Art

2 Symbolics of Information e.g. maths, linguistics, logic

Zetetic Education

10 Disseminative Area e.g. education, library science

Isomorphic Symbolics

3 Hylenergetics e.g. physics, chemistry, astronomy

Social Ethics

9 Regulative Area e.g. political science, economics

Biophysics, Biochemistry

4 Biological Area e.g. botany, zoology, cytology

Pacifics

8 Pronoetics e.g. agriculture, medicine

Physiological Psychology

5 Psychology e.g. animal, developmental, abnormal

Prognostics

7 Exeligmology e.g. cosmology, evolution, history

Anthropology

Social Psychology

6 Sociology e.g. ecology, ethnology, demography

The Unknowables
Knowables not yet known
KNOWLEDGE

J. Tykociner, 'Zetetics and Areas of Knowledge', in S. M. Elam (ed.), *Education and the Structure of Knowledge,* ch. 4 (Phi Delta Kappa, Rand McNally, Skokie, Ill., 1964).

Appendix

Notes on some of the principal authors cited in this book

Benjamin Bloom, of the University of Chicago, was the leader of a distinguished team of American academics which worked, between 1949 and 1953, on devising a classification system for educational objectives, their principal interest being to improve the quality of college examining. They agreed not to get involved in value judgements about objectives, but to devise a scheme which would be 'neutral with respect to educational principles and philosophies'. This remarkable work claims to classify the 'intended behaviour of students', how well they perform the intended skills. Bloom himself edited the first volume, *The Cognitive Domain,* which was published in 1956; the second volume, *The Affective Domain,* edited by another member of the team, David Krathwohl of Michigan State University, did not appear until 1964. Volume III has not appeared at the time of writing (1974).

1971 saw the publication of Bloom's *Handbook on Formative and Summative Evaluation of Student Behaviour,* a weighty and impressive tome, packed with information and suggestions.

Jerome Bruner was Professor of Psychology at Harvard University in the 1960's and is now (1974) Watts Professor of Experimental Psychology at Oxford. He is best known for his two books *The Process of Education* (1966) and *Toward a Theory of Instruction* (1968). The main burden of these books is, perhaps, that important concepts can be taught in a simple form even to young children. In the later book he illustrates this claim with reference to mathematics, and also to social studies. His ideas have taken concrete form in the celebrated curriculum, 'Man: a Course of Study', which is now beginning to be taught in British schools. Latterly his writings have suggested a less optimistic view, and the problems of motivation, of poverty, of deschooling seem to figure more in his thinking. His most recent publication is *Beyond the Information Given* (1974), a collection of his more celebrated papers.

Robert Mager is an American writer the best known of whose books, *Preparing Instructional Objectives* (1962) and *Developing Attitude toward Learning* (1968), are compulsive reading, being short, clear and amusing. The former, first published as *Preparing Objectives for programmed instruction,* is presented in the form of a programmed text, and reflects the enthusiasm of the programmed learning movement of the early 1960's. All his writing assumes the value of precisely stated behavioural objectives stated in operational terms; the pendulum has begun to swing back against this approach, but the books remain refreshing reading.

Philip Phenix, Professor of Philosophy and Education at Teachers College, Columbia University, is perhaps best known for his *Realms of Meaning* (1964) which provides an extremely interesting and useful classification of human knowledge into six main categories: symbolics, empirics, esthetics, synnoetics, ethics, synoptics. Representative ideas from these categories should be the basis for a balanced curriculum. The book gives a remarkably clear outline map, never becoming too abstruse to follow. Its style is readable and succinct, and it is beautifully constructed. As an account of the different 'ways of knowing' which education aims to pass on it takes some beating.

D. K. Wheeler was a Fulbright research scholar in the United States and Professor of Curriculum Development in Beirut in the early 1960's. His book *Curriculum Process,* published in 1967 when he was Senior Lecturer at the University of Western Australia, has been influential largely because it was virtually the first account to be published in Britain of the orthodox approach to curriculum development which has come to be known as rational curriculum planning. Its timely appearance and comprehensive coverage have made it one of the standard works. It is unmistakably American in flavour, and its debt to writers such as Bloom, Taba and Tyler is very obvious; but it is written in such general terms that it is easily applied to any country's curriculum development problems, and it does contain some references to the British situation such as the Newsom and Crowther Reports.